MEXICAN IMMIGRATION

LeeAnne Gelletly

THE CHANGING Face of North America:
IMMIGRATION SINCE 1965

Asylees

Chinese Immigration

Cuban Immigration

Deported Aliens

Filipino Immigration

Haitian Immigration

Immigration from Central America

Immigration from the Dominican Republic

Immigration from the Former Yugoslavia

Immigration from the Middle East

Immigration from South America

Indian Immigration

Korean Immigration

Mexican Immigration

Refugees

Vietnamese Immigration

MEXICAN IMMIGRATION

LeeAnne Gelletly

MASON CREST PUBLISHERS
PHILADELPHIA

Produced by OTTN Publishing, Stockton, New Jersey

Mason Crest Publishers
370 Reed Road
Broomall, PA 19008
www.masoncrest.com

First printing

1 3 5 7 9 8 6 4 2

Library of Congress Cataloging-in-Publication Data

Gelletly, LeeAnne.
 Mexican immigration / LeeAnne Gelletly.
  p. cm. — (The changing face of North America)
Summary: An overview of immigration from Mexico to the United States and Canada since the 1960s, when immigration laws were changed to permit greater numbers of people to enter these countries.
Includes bibliographical references and index.
 ISBN 1-59084-680-X
1. Mexican Americans—History—20th century—Juvenile literature. 2 Mexicans—Canada—History—20th century—Juvenile literature. 3. Immigrants—United States—History—20th century—Juvenile literature.
4. Immigrants—Canada—History—20th century—Juvenile literature. 5. Mexico—Emigration and immigration—History—20th century—Juvenile literature. 6. United States—Emigration and immigration—History—20th century—Juvenile literature. 7. Canada—Emigration and immigration—History—20th century—Juvenile literature. [1. Mexican Americans—History—20th century. 2. Mexicans—Canada—History—20th century. 3. Immigrants—United States—History—20th century. 4. Immigrants—Canada—History—20th century. 5. Mexico—Emigration and immigration—History—20th century. 6. United States—Emigration and immigration—History—20th century. 7. Canada—Emigration and immigration—History—20th century.] I. Title. II. Series.
 E184.M5G45 2004
 304.8'73072—dc22

                                                2003013260

THE **CHANGING**
Face of North America:
IMMIGRATION SINCE 1965

CONTENTS

Introduction
Senator Edward M. Kennedy   **6**

Foreword
Marian L. Smith   **8**
Peter A. Hammerschmidt   **11**

Mexican Americans   **15**

The Struggle to Provide a Living   **27**

Immigration to the North   **39**

Making a New Home   **59**

**Choosing Between the
Old and the New**   **67**

Problems Facing Mexican Immigrants   **79**

**The Growing Influence
of Mexican Americans**   **91**

Famous Mexican Americans/Canadians **100**

Glossary   **103**

Further Reading   **104**

Internet Resources   **105**

Index   **106**

INTRODUCTION

THE CHANGING FACE OF AMERICA

By Senator Edward M. Kennedy

America is proud of its heritage and history as a nation of immigrants, and my own family is an example. All eight of my great-grandparents were immigrants who left Ireland a century and a half ago, when that land was devastated by the massive famine caused by the potato blight. When I was a young boy, my grandfather used to take me down to the docks in Boston and regale me with stories about the Great Famine and the waves of Irish immigrants who came to America seeking a better life. He talked of how the Irish left their marks in Boston and across the nation, enduring many hardships and harsh discrimination, but also building the railroads, digging the canals, settling the West, and filling the factories of a growing America. According to one well-known saying of the time, "under every railroad tie, an Irishman is buried."

America was the promised land for them, as it has been for so many other immigrants who have found shelter, hope, opportunity, and freedom. Immigrants have always been an indispensable part of our nation. They have contributed immensely to our communities, created new jobs and whole new industries, served in our armed forces, and helped make America the continuing land of promise that it is today.

The inspiring poem by Emma Lazarus, inscribed on the pedestal of the Statue of Liberty in New York Harbor, is America's welcome to all immigrants:

Give me your tired, your poor,
Your huddled masses yearning to breathe free,
The wretched refuse of your teeming shore,
Send these, the homeless, tempest-tossed, to me:
I lift my lamp beside the golden door.

The period since September 11, 2001, has been particularly challenging for immigrants. Since the horrifying terrorist attacks, there has been a resurgence of anti-immigrant attitudes and behavior. We all agree that our borders must be safe and secure. Yet, at the same time, we must safeguard the entry of the millions of persons who come to the United States legally each year as immigrants, visitors, scholars, students, and workers. The "golden door" must stay open. We must recognize that immigration is not the problem—terrorism is. We must identify and isolate the terrorists, and not isolate America.

One of my most important responsibilities in the Senate is the preservation of basic rights and basic fairness in the application of our immigration laws, so that new generations of immigrants in our own time and for all time will have the same opportunity that my great-grandparents had when they arrived in America.

Immigration is beneficial for the United States and for countries throughout the world. It is no coincidence that two hundred years ago, our nations' founders chose *E Pluribus Unum*—"out of many, one"—as America's motto. These words, chosen by Benjamin Franklin, John Adams, and Thomas Jefferson, refer to the ideal that separate colonies can be transformed into one united nation. Today, this ideal has come to apply to individuals as well. Our diversity is our strength. We are a nation of immigrants, and we always will be.

THE CHANGING FACE OF THE UNITED STATES

Marian L. Smith, historian
U.S. Immigration and Naturalization Service

Americans commonly assume that immigration today is very different than immigration of the past. The immigrants themselves appear
to be unlike immigrants of earlier eras. Their language, their dress,
their food, and their ways seem strange. At times people fear too
many of these new immigrants will destroy the America they know.
But has anything really changed? Do new immigrants have any
different effect on America than old immigrants a century ago? Is the
American fear of too much immigration a new development? Do
immigrants really change America more than America changes the
immigrants? The very subject of immigration raises many questions.

In the United States, immigration is more than a chapter in a history book. It is a continuous thread that links the present moment to
the first settlers on North American shores. From the first colonists'
arrival until today, immigrants have been met by Americans who both
welcomed and feared them. Immigrant contributions were always
welcome—on the farm, in the fields, and in the factories. Welcoming
the poor, the persecuted, and the "huddled masses" became an
American principle. Beginning with the original Pilgrims' flight from
religious persecution in the 1600s, through the Irish migration to
escape starvation in the 1800s, to the relocation of Central
Americans seeking refuge from civil wars in the 1980s and 1990s, the
United States has considered itself a haven for the destitute and the
oppressed.

But there was also concern that immigrants would not adopt American ways, habits, or language. Too many immigrants might overwhelm America. If so, the dream of the Founding Fathers for United States government and society would be destroyed. For this reason, throughout American history some have argued that limiting or ending immigration is our patriotic duty. Benjamin Franklin feared there were so many German immigrants in Pennsylvania the Colonial Legislature would begin speaking German. "Progressive" leaders of the early 1900s feared that immigrants who could not read and understand the English language were not only exploited by "big business," but also served as the foundation for "machine politics" that undermined the U.S. Constitution. This theme continues today, usually voiced by those who bear no malice toward immigrants but who want to preserve American ideals.

Have immigrants changed? In colonial days, when most colonists were of English descent, they considered Germans, Swiss, and French immigrants as different. They were not "one of us" because they spoke a different language. Generations later, Americans of German or French descent viewed Polish, Italian, and Russian immigrants as strange. They were not "like us" because they had a different religion, or because they did not come from a tradition of constitutional government. Recently, Americans of Polish or Italian descent have seen Nicaraguan, Pakistani, or Vietnamese immigrants as too different to be included. It has long been said of American immigration that the latest ones to arrive usually want to close the door behind them.

It is important to remember that fear of individual immigrant groups seldom lasted, and always lessened. Benjamin Franklin's anxiety over German immigrants disappeared after those immigrants' sons and daughters helped the nation gain independence in the Revolutionary War. The Irish of the mid-1800s were among the most hated immigrants, but today we all wear green on St. Patrick's Day. While a century ago it was feared that Italian and other Catholic immigrants would vote as directed by the Pope, today that controversy is only a vague memory. Unfortunately, some ethnic groups continue their efforts to earn acceptance. The African

Americans' struggle continues, and some Asian Americans, whose families have been in America for generations, are the victims of current anti-immigrant sentiment.

Time changes both immigrants and America. Each wave of new immigrants, with their strange language and habits, eventually grows old and passes away. Their American-born children speak English. The immigrants' grandchildren are completely American. The strange foods of their ancestors—spaghetti, baklava, hummus, or tofu—become common in any American restaurant or grocery store. Much of what the immigrants brought to these shores is lost, principally their language. And what is gained becomes as American as St. Patrick's Day, Hanukkah, or Cinco de Mayo, and we forget that it was once something foreign.

Recent immigrants are all around us. They come from every corner of the earth to join in the American Dream. They will continue to help make the American Dream a reality, just as all the immigrants who came before them have done.

FOREWORD

THE CHANGING FACE OF CANADA

Peter A. Hammerschmidt
First Secretary of the Canadian Mission to the United Nations

Throughout Canada's history, immigration has shaped and defined the very character of Canadian society. The migration of peoples from every part of the world into Canada has profoundly changed the way we look, speak, eat, and live. Through close and distant relatives who left their lands in search of a better life, all Canadians have links to immigrant pasts. We are a nation built by and of immigrants.

Two parallel forces have shaped the history of Canadian immigration. The enormous diversity of Canada's immigrant population is the most obvious. In the beginning came the enterprising settlers of the "New World," the French and English colonists. Soon after came the Scottish, Irish, and Northern and Central European farmers of the 1700s and 1800s. As the country expanded westward during the mid-1800s, migrant workers began arriving from China, Japan, and other Asian countries. And the turbulent twentieth century brought an even greater variety of immigrants to Canada, from the Caribbean, Africa, India, and Southeast Asia.

So while English- and French-Canadians are the largest ethnic groups in the country today, neither group alone represents a majority of the population. A large and vibrant multicultural mix makes up the rest, particularly in Canada's major cities. Toronto, Vancouver, and Montreal alone are home to people from over 200 ethnic groups!

Less obvious but equally important in the evolution of Canadian immigration has been hope. The promise of a better life lured Europeans and Americans seeking cheap (sometimes even free) farmland. Thousands of Scots and Irish arrived to escape grinding poverty and starvation. Others came for freedom, to escape religious and political persecution. Canada has long been a haven to the world's dispossessed and disenfranchised—Dutch and German farmers cast out for their religious beliefs, black slaves fleeing the United States, and political refugees of despotic regimes in Europe, Africa, Asia, and South America.

The two forces of diversity and hope, so central to Canada's past, also shaped the modern era of Canadian immigration. Following the Second World War, Canada drew heavily on these influences to forge trailblazing immigration initiatives.

The catalyst for change was the adoption of the Canadian Bill of Rights in 1960. Recognizing its growing diversity and Canadians' changing attitudes towards racism, the government passed a federal statute barring discrimination on the grounds of race, national origin, color, religion, or sex. Effectively rejecting the discriminatory elements in Canadian immigration policy, the Bill of Rights forced the introduction of a new policy in 1962. The focus of immigration abruptly switched from national origin to the individual's potential contribution to Canadian society. The door to Canada was now open to every corner of the world.

Welcoming those seeking new hopes in a new land has also been a feature of Canadian immigration in the modern era. The focus on economic immigration has increased along with Canada's steadily growing economy, but political immigration has also been encouraged. Since 1945, Canada has admitted tens of thousands of displaced persons, including Jewish Holocaust survivors, victims of Soviet crackdowns in Hungary and Czechoslovakia, and refugees from political upheaval in Uganda, Chile, and Vietnam.

Prior to 1978, however, these political refugees were admitted as an exception to normal immigration procedures. That year, Canada

revamped its refugee policy with a new Immigration Act that explicit-
ly affirmed Canada's commitment to the resettlement of refugees
from oppression. Today, the admission of refugees remains a central
part of Canadian immigration law and regulations.

Amendments to economic and political immigration policy
continued during the 1980s and 1990s, refining further the bold
steps taken during the modern era. Together, these initiatives have
turned Canada into one of the world's few truly multicultural states.

Unlike the process of assimilation into a "melting pot" of cultures,
immigrants to Canada are more likely to retain their cultural identity,
beliefs, and practices. This is the source of some of Canada's
greatest strengths as a society. And as a truly multicultural nation,
diversity is not seen as a threat to Canadian identity. Quite the
contrary—diversity *is* Canadian identity.

1 MEXICAN AMERICANS

More than 20 million people living in the United States today claim Mexican heritage. Some of them can trace their ancestors, originally from Mexico or Spain, to the early settlers of the present-day U.S. Southwest. Others came later, in waves of migration that occurred throughout the 20th century. Still others arrived a decade or two ago, while some entered the country only recently.

Most northward migration from Mexico has ended within the boundaries of the United States. As of 1950, only a few Mexicans had chosen to live as far north as Canada, and these were mostly the Mexican-born children of Canadian Mennonites who had migrated to northern Mexico during the early 20th century. However, beginning in the 1970s, growing numbers of Mexicans were making Canada their home. According to the country's 2001 Census, over 36,000 people of Mexican descent had settled there, mostly in the urban areas of Ontario, British Columbia, Quebec, and Alberta. Compared with the United States, Canada is home to relatively few Mexicans. Mexicans and Mexican Americans make up one of the largest and most rapidly growing minority groups in the United States.

The Mexican People

Directly south of the United States, separated for about 1,250 miles (2,012 kilometers) by the twisting Rio Grande, lies

◄ A group of men approach the U.S. border at Agua Prieta, Mexico. In 2000, almost 8 million Mexican-born people were living in the United States—more than one-quarter of the foreign-born population. The Mexican population in Canada has been expanding in recent decades, though it is still much lower than in the United States.

the country of Mexico, made up of 31 states. Mexico consists mostly of desert and mountainous terrain, with only an estimated 10 percent of the land good for farming. Its population totals more than 100 million people.

About 60 percent of the Mexican population is *mestizo*, the Spanish word meaning "mixed." Mestizos have a combined Native American and Spanish background. Mexico's original settlers, Native Americans, were conquered by Spain in 16th century and were ruled by that country for almost 300 years. During that time Spanish settlers brought their language, religious faith, and traditions, which became incorporated into the mestizo culture.

About 15 to 30 percent of Mexicans are Native Americans, and a much smaller number are of European or African

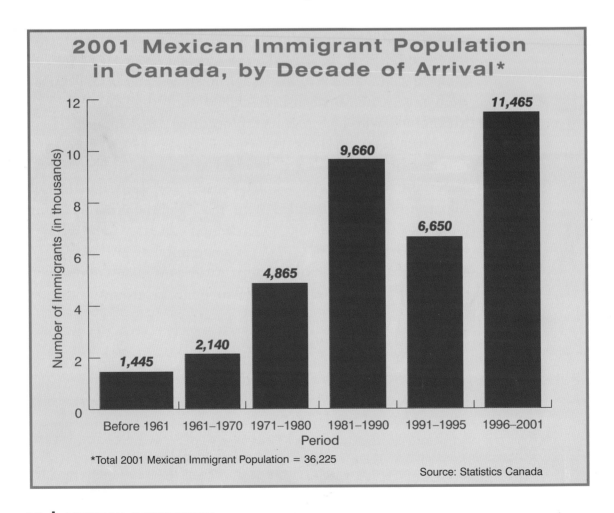

2001 Mexican Immigrant Population in Canada, by Decade of Arrival*

*Total 2001 Mexican Immigrant Population = 36,225

Source: Statistics Canada

descent. Although the Mexican people may be diverse in appearance and culture, most are united by their Spanish language, their Catholic faith, and a strong sense of family and community.

Part of the Hispanic Culture

Since the 1960s, the U.S. Bureau of the Census (the government agency that records how many people live in the United States) has grouped all Spanish-speaking people together as *Hispanic*. This category includes people from Mexico, as well as from Puerto Rico, Cuba, the Dominican Republic, and many Latin American countries. For the most part, the term is not used in Spanish-speaking countries.

Until recently Hispanics were the second-largest minority group in the United States, smaller only than the African American population. But in mid-2001, according to the U.S. Census Bureau, Hispanics became the largest minority group. The number of Hispanics living in the United States grew from 22.4 million (9 percent of the population) in 1990 to 35.3 million (12 percent) in 2000. By mid-2001, the Census reported, the number of Hispanics living in the United States totaled 37 million (13 percent). More than half of this group has its roots in Mexico.

Because the terms *Hispanic* and *Latino* refer to people from so many different countries, races, and cultures, some Mexican Americans prefer to refer to themselves by other names that clearly define who they are. For example, Mexican Americans from Texas are Tejanos; in California they are Californios. During the 1950s and 1960s, many young Mexican Americans preferred the term *Chicano*, a shortened version of *Mexicano*, although their elders disapproved of the word, which was previously used as an ethnic slur. But for younger generations, *Chicano* became a source of ethnic pride that acknowledged their connection to Mexico.

Mexican Americans may also belong to other racial groups (Caucasians, Native Americans, Africans, or a mixture).

However, they proudly consider themselves members of *La raza*, the same cultural and ethnic group whose heart lies in Mexico.

The Mexican and Mexican American Population

Demographers (people who study human population statistics) have developed different ways to count immigrants. For example, researchers trying to describe the Mexican population in the United States may look at the number of Mexican-born people residing in the country, the number of Mexicans who legally immigrate to the United States in a particular year, or the number of people living in the country who report Mexican heritage.

Mexican-born residents are first-generation immigrants, those

A Mexican family runs across the border between Tijuana, Mexico, and San Diego, California. Researchers estimated in 2002 that 3 to 4 million Mexicans living in the United States did not have lawful immigration status.

who left the country of their birth to move to a new land. Census statistics of the foreign-born population indicate a strong, steady increase in the number of Mexican-born immigrants living in the United States. The total was about 576,000 in 1960; almost 760,000 in 1970; over 2 million in 1980; over 4 million in 1990; and about 8 million in 2000. In 2000 the U.S. Bureau of the Census reported that Mexicans accounted for more than one-quarter of the foreign-born population of the United States.

For decades, Mexicans have formed the largest group of legal immigrants (people lawfully admitted for permanent residence) to the United States. In 1960 about 32,000 Mexicans legally immigrated to the United States. In 1970 that number approached 65,000. It surpassed 100,000 in 1980, approached 174,000 in 2000, and was over 219,000 in 2002. Throughout the 1990s and into 2000 Mexicans accounted for approximately 20 percent of all legal immigrants.

However, Mexicans have also accounted for a large percentage of undocumented immigrants entering the United States. (These are immigrants without legal paperwork, also referred to as "illegal immigrants.") Exact numbers are impossible to determine, but official estimates indicate that from 1960 to 1980 illegal Mexican migration rose steadily. Government officials estimate that since the 1980s about 300,000 undocumented Mexican immigrants have entered the United States each year. As of 2002, researchers estimated that about 8 million people were living in the United States without lawful immigration status—and that 3 to 4 million of them were from Mexico.

In the U.S. Census, Mexican American residents are also counted by ethnic background, which includes U.S. citizens whose families have lived in the country for generations, as well as recent immigrants. According to the 2000 Census, more than 20 million Mexicans and Mexican Americans, or 7.3 percent of the total population, live in the United States today.

Mexican American Culture

Mexican Americans have contributed much to American culture, becoming politically active during the Chicano movement of the 1960s and in the years since. This movement united a large number of Mexican Americans seeking to obtain equal rights in politics, education, and the workplace through labor strikes and peaceful protest. During this time activist César Chávez organized farmworkers, while students protested the poor conditions in inner-city schools and U.S. involvement in the Vietnam War. The Chicano movement represented more than a group's protests against discrimination and inequality; it also symbolized a new pride in Mexican identity.

That pride soon translated into the political action of the Chicano movement, as Mexican Americans organized voter

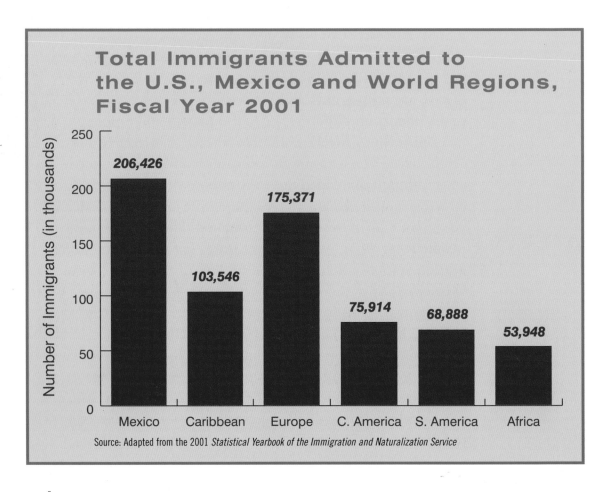

Total Immigrants Admitted to the U.S., Mexico and World Regions, Fiscal Year 2001

Source: Adapted from the 2001 *Statistical Yearbook of the Immigration and Naturalization Service*

Representative Henry B. González of Texas was a leading advocate for Latino causes. In 1976 he co-founded the Hispanic Congressional Caucus, an organization working to ensure that legislators debated the issues pertaining to Mexican Americans and other Latinos.

registration drives and supported Hispanic candidates. Many Mexican Americans entered politics during this time. They ran for school boards, city councils, county councils, and state and federal legislatures. In 1974 two Mexican Americans were elected state governors: Jerry Apodaca in New Mexico and Raul Castro in Arizona. By 1980, six Hispanic Americans were serving in the U.S. Congress. By the late 1990s, that number had increased to 20.

In 1976 U.S. Representatives Henry B. González of Texas and Edward R. Roybal of California founded the Hispanic Congressional Caucus to ensure that the Latino voice was heard in the legislative debate. In 1981 Henry G. Cisneros became the first Mexican American–elected mayor of a major

U.S. city, San Antonio; he later served as secretary of housing and urban development under President Bill Clinton. Through the years other Mexican Americans have served in cabinet positions for various presidents: Katherine Ortega became U.S. treasurer under President Ronald Reagan; Manuel Lujan Jr., interior secretary under President George H. W. Bush; and former Denver mayor Fredęrico Peña, secretary of transportation and energy under Clinton.

Some believe that the Chicano movement also helped encourage Mexican American writing. One representative work from early in the movement is Rodolfo "Corky" Gonzales's poem, *I Am Joaquin* (1967). Other distinguished writers of essays, fiction, and poetry include Rodolfo A. Anaya, Sandra Cisneros, Ana Castillo, Richard Rodriguez, and Francisco Jiménez. Countless more have contributed to the growing field of Chicano literature, which is studied in universities across the United States.

During the 1990s, more doors opened to Hispanics,

Born in Mexico, Salma Hayek is widely recognized for her portrayals of Mexican and Mexican American characters. Her title performance in *Frida*, a biopic about the revolutionary Mexican painter Frida Kahlo, earned her an Oscar nomination in 2003.

allowing Mexican and Mexican American artists to make inroads in the entertainment industry. Latin-flavored singles and albums climbed the charts during the 1990s, with major contributions from Mexican-born guitarist Carlos Santana and Tejano pop-star Selena. The beginning of the 21st century saw more Mexican Americans portrayed on network television and in movie theaters, with stars such as Mexican American actor Edward James Olmos and Mexican-born actress Salma Hayek.

Mexico has continually produced American sports stars such as baseball pitchers Fernando Valenzela and Ted Higuera. Descendants of Mexican immigrants, such as boxer Oscar de La Hoya and speed skater Derek Parra, have won Olympic gold for the United States.

The Mexican influence has also reached into the kitchens and dining rooms of Americans. Chili, tacos, burritos, and enchiladas have become commonplace snacks and meals throughout America. Frozen versions of these dishes are easily found in mainstream grocery stores and fast-food restaurants, along with tortillas and taco chips. In the 1990s, salsa—a spicy tomato-based sauce—had become such a staple in many households that its sales surpassed those of catsup.

Economic Contributions to the U.S. Economy

However, one of the biggest impacts that Mexican immigrants have had on the United States is cumulative—years and years of hard work in jobs often shunned by others. These jobs, many in the fields of agriculture and industry, can be low-paying and low-prestige. Immigrant workers have picked lettuce in California, apples in Washington, and oranges in Florida. They have harvested mushrooms in Pennsylvania, tobacco in North Carolina, and cotton in Texas; cleaned fish in Alaska; sewn garments in New York City and Los Angeles; and worked in the slaughterhouses of Iowa and Kansas.

For decades, Mexican immigrants have provided an industrious workforce for agriculture and business throughout

César Chávez: Fighting for the Rights of Migrant Farmworkers

For decades Mexican migrant workers endured difficult living and working conditions. Housed in shacks without running water or electricity, farmworkers toiled 7 days a week for 15 cents an hour.

During the 1960s, a former migrant worker named César Chávez sought to bring about change through labor union action. In 1962 Chávez and activist Delores Huerta founded the National Farmworkers Association (NFWA) in Delano, California. Three years later Chávez organized a strike against grape growers in Delano County. This protest eventually evolved into a nationwide grape boycott that lasted five years. Its resolution brought about improved housing, health benefits, and wages for workers. In 1966, the NFWA merged with another union, creating the United Farmworkers (UFW), AFL-CIO.

Chávez led other labor actions against California lettuce growers, as well as organizing additional grape boycotts. He served as head of the UFW until his death in April 1993. A steadfast believer in the effectiveness of nonviolent protest, Chávez was posthumously honored with the Presidential Medal of Freedom, the highest civilian honor in the United States, in 1994.

the United States. Many big American industries—construction companies, nurseries and fruit growers, meatpacking and poultry companies—have relied on these workers in great numbers. Their efforts helped the U.S. economy grow during the second half of the 20th century.

During the 1990s, the United States saw an influx of immigration from Mexico. Many of these newcomers, according to a 2002 study by Northeastern University's Center for Market Studies, filled jobs as private domestic workers, machine operators, and laborers that helped the United States prevent serious labor shortages. The Northeastern University study reported that immigrants provided 50 percent of America's labor-force growth in the 1990s. Labor-force growth is an essential element, along with productivity, in spurring a nation's economic growth and thereby raising standards of living.

Other Mexican immigrants have traveled further up the economic ladder, many as small-business owners. Many of their entrepreneurial shops and companies have contributed to the revitalization of blighted inner-city areas, while providing specialized products and services for Latinos. The successful growth of these businesses fills the needs of an ever-growing Hispanic population.

2 THE STRUGGLE TO PROVIDE A LIVING

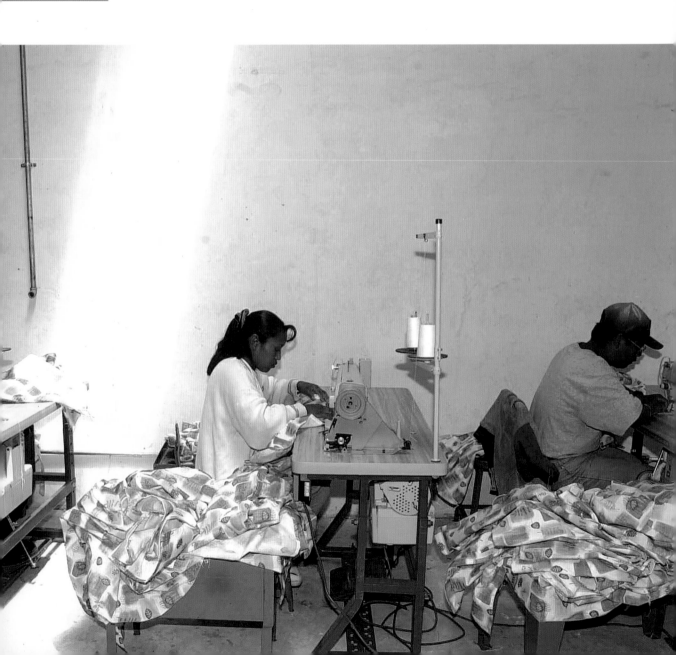

For most people, the decision to leave the land of their birth does not come easily. Sometimes extreme events such as political upheaval or national disasters leave victims no choice but to migrate. In a few instances during the past century, Mexican migrations have resulted because of war and catastrophe. In 1910, a bloody revolution drove millions of Mexican refugees to safety in the north. And in 1985 thousands left Mexico City in search of new homes and lives when a major earthquake killed 10,000 people and destroyed blocks of buildings. But for the most part, migration from Mexico has resulted because people were trying to escape from poverty.

Economic Migration

The 2,000-mile (3,219-km) border between Mexico and the United States stretches east to west, from near Brownsville, Texas (on the Gulf coast) to Tijuana, Mexico (at the beaches of the Pacific Ocean). This line separates two worlds—one of extreme poverty and the other of great wealth. As a developing country, Mexico has had trouble providing jobs and economic opportunities for its people, a majority of whom are poor. According to World Bank 2002 estimates, 40 percent of Mexicans earn less than two dollars a day (less than $400 a year). Meanwhile to the north, in the United States and Canada, the per capita income is over $34,000. With such a large income gap, many Mexicans choose to immigrate to the

◀ Mexican workers sew women's garments in one of the many maquiladoras found just south of the U.S.–Mexico border. These U.S.–owned factories employ a great segment of the Mexican workforce, though laborers are attracted to the less-grueling, higher-paying jobs that are often found north of the border.

north in order to find higher-wage jobs and better opportunities than they can find in Mexico.

A busy intersection in Mexico City, the capital of Mexico. During the country's recession in the 1980s, many city workers, along with rural laborers, lost their jobs and migrated to the United States in search of work.

Mexico's Efforts to Create Jobs

Starting around the 1940s, the Mexican government began taking steps to reduce the economy's dependence on agriculture and mining. By industrializing the country, the government hoped, more jobs would be created for the unemployed (out of work) and underemployed (working only part-time when the person wants to work full-time or working at a job requiring fewer skills than a person is trained for).

Among these efforts was the creation in 1965 of industrial zones along the border with the United States. In these areas, foreign companies could establish assembly plants, called maquiladoras, that had special privileges. Factory owners would pay minimal taxes and utility costs. The government would provide subsidies and drop import tariffs on materials coming to the plants. The finished, manufactured products would then be shipped back north. By promoting intense industrial growth, Mexican officials hoped the country could benefit from foreign investment while reducing unemployment.

Lured by an abundant labor supply of ready workers, American companies, as well as firms from other countries, built maquiladoras all along these industrial zones. In 1970 more than 200 of these factories had been built, with about 19,000 employees. By the end of 1990 there were almost 2,000 factories, employing 500,000. And by the late 1990s more than 2,500 maquiladoras provided jobs for over one million workers living along the border.

Most maquiladora work was hard, usually consisting of long hours of repetitive work. The assembly plants tended to hire young women, who accepted lower pay than men. Wages ranged from $3 to $9 a day, which was much lower than salaries for comparable work in the United States. While northern Mexico was offering much-needed job opportunities, just over the border workers could find much higher-paying jobs.

Meanwhile the maquiladora program created boomtowns, as Mexicans from central and southern Mexico flocked to the northern border in search of jobs. But the program did not solve Mexico's unemployment problem. By the early 1980s, 48 percent of Mexicans were unemployed or underemployed.

In addition, the growth in Mexico's border towns brought a new challenge: how to provide for the overwhelming number of residents. Many lived in shantytowns, called *colonias*, without electricity or water. Raw sewage and waste from both residential and industrial areas flowed into nearby rivers, while industrial toxins were disposed of along roadsides. The maquiladora industry created environmental problems that the Mexican government did not have the resources to prevent.

A Faltering Economy

During the 1970s, Mexico entered a brief period of prosperity, resulting in part from the discovery of major petroleum deposits on the coast of the Gulf of Mexico. Soon the country became a major exporter to the United States. Anticipating large revenues because of the high price of oil, the Mexican government borrowed heavily from banks in the United States and Europe to cover costs for major construction projects. Then in the early 1980s, the price of oil fell and Mexico found itself with a large foreign debt it could not repay.

The resulting economic recession cost many Mexican workers their jobs. Many workers who were better educated and lived in the city joined the ranks of rural Mexicans migrating north in search of jobs during the 1980s. The workers in the city, however, were seeking non-agricultural jobs.

Additional foreign investment and rescheduling of payment dates for loans helped Mexico's economy improve during the late 1980s and early 1990s. Other economic reforms made under President Carlos Salinas de Gotari (1988–94) and President Ernesto Zedillo (1994–2000) helped as well. Salinas and the ruling party, the Partido Revolucionario Institucional (PRI), worked to improve the economy by dropping tariffs that had protected its own industries but had also made them less efficient. Zedillo also privatized state-owned industries, meaning that banks, utilities, and airlines that had been run by the Mexican government were sold to privately owned industries. However, the government still maintained a significant impact on the economy—in the minds of many observers, a negative impact. A large number of Mexicans viewed high-level Mexican government officials as corrupt, and many scandals over the years seemed to bear this out.

North American Free Trade Agreement

The success of Salinas's economic reforms was complemented by a free-trade zone agreement established among the North American countries of Canada, the United States, and Mexico.

Mexican president Carlos Salinas de Gotari, who led the country between 1988 and 1994, signed the landmark North American Free Trade Agreement (NAFTA) in 1991. The agreement, which lowered the prices of imports to Mexico, also sought to stem the tide of undocumented immigrants entering the U.S.

Called the North American Free Trade Agreement (NAFTA), this accord aimed to facilitate the movement of goods, services, and money across borders by gradually eliminating (over a 10-year period) tariffs and other trade barriers. On December 17, 1992, U.S. President George H. W. Bush, Canadian prime minister Brian Mulroney, and Mexican president Carlos Salinas de Gotari signed NAFTA, which was implemented in January 1994.

By helping to prevent practices that artificially raise the prices of goods and services imported into Mexico, NAFTA would help Mexican consumers. Similarly, imports into the United States from Canada and Mexico would benefit U.S. consumers through lower prices bred by greater competition and the absence of tariffs (taxes that governments levy on certain foreign goods). Despite these benefits to consumers in all three countries, the agreement was controversial in the United States. Many U.S. residents feared NAFTA would encourage more U.S. companies to move south of the border. Others supported the agreement, believing it would also open up new markets for U.S. companies to sell their goods and services. Some also argued that it would boost Mexico's economy and result in more jobs for the country, allowing it to better provide for its people. A larger middle class of Mexican consumers could create new markets for American goods, and potentially reduce the number of undocumented immigrants coming for jobs in the north.

Continuing Economic Troubles

Some Mexicans worried that the elimination of tariffs on goods coming from the United States would be bad for the agricultural industry, which is located mostly in southern

Members of the Ejército Zapatista de Liberación Nacional (EZLN), a rebel group, gather before a meeting. The Zapatistas, who united to fight the unjust practices of large farm owners, briefly took over the state capital of San Cristobal de Las Casas in 1994 before government forces crushed the rebellion.

The First Mexican Americans

In 1848 the Mexican government signed the Treaty of Guadalupe Hidalgo, which outlined terms ending the Mexican War (1846–48). The pact gave away a large section of territory claimed by Mexico (present-day Texas, California, Nevada, and Utah, as well as parts of Colorado, New Mexico, and Wyoming). Later, the United States paid Mexico $15 million for the land, and in 1853, another $10 million (the Gadsden Purchase) for southern Arizona and New Mexico.

These transactions affected approximately 80,000 Mexican settlers and their descendants living in what had been northern Mexico but was now the U.S. Southwest. As a popular expression of Tejanos goes, "We never crossed a border. The border crossed us."

According to the terms of the Treaty of Guadalupe Hidalgo, these first Mexican Americans were granted U.S. citizenship and legal protection. However, the Mexican and American cultures did not mesh easily. Within just a few years the English-language U.S. courts and some disreputable American speculators had cheated Mexican landowners out of large tracts of property. By the late 1800s the majority of these first Mexican Americans were landless second-class citizens living in poverty and working at low-wage jobs.

Mexico, home to many Native Americans. These fears, along with growing discontent over poverty and the unfair practices of large farmers and ranchers, sparked an uprising in Mexico's southernmost state of Chiapas in 1994. A group calling itself the Ejército Zapatista de Liberación Nacional (EZLN) took over the state capital of San Cristobal de Las Casas, demanding better social and economic opportunities. Although quickly routed by government troops, the EZLN continued to rebel against the Mexican government, creating ongoing political turmoil in Chiapas.

In 1994, just at the beginning of President Zedillo's term of office, the Mexican government was forced to devalue the peso, the Mexican monetary unit, to reflect its true value against the American dollar. The value of the peso fell so low that foreign investors pulled their money out of Mexico. The

President Vicente Fox of Mexico, who began his term in December 2000, speaks before the U.S. Congress. Among the major issues during Fox's initial years in office were immigration reform and the creation of economic incentives for Mexican workers to remain in the country.

nation suffered its worst economic recession in 50 years as inflation rates soared as much as 200 percent. A 1996 study by the Colegio de México reported that 80 percent of the population lived in poverty.

Mexico's economy began to recover after the country received emergency loans from the U.S. government and the World Bank. From 1994 to 1995 the country's gross domestic product (GDP, the value of all the goods and services produced in a nation) had declined by 6.2 percent. (A healthy economy should have a steadily increasing GDP.) But in 2000 the GDP showed a healthy 6.9 percent growth rate. The following year the GDP fell slightly, but the economy appeared to be stabilizing and the value of peso gained slightly against the dollar.

By the beginning of the 21st century, economists reported that Mexico's trade with the U.S. and Canada had tripled since implementation of NAFTA. These exports by companies in Mexico helped create new jobs for Mexicans and benefited American and Canadian consumers by keeping prices low.

A major political shift in Mexico took place in 2000. For the first time in 71 years, the incumbent party—the Partido Revolucionario Institucional (PRI)—lost the presidency. Mexican voters elected Vicente Fox of the Partido Acción Nacional (PAN). Sworn into office on December 1, 2000, the new Mexican president promised to strengthen ties with foreign investors. He also planned to turn his attention to the millions of Mexican immigrants working and making their home in the United States.

The Typical Migrant

In a 2001 study of Mexican immigration to the United States published in the *Latin American Research Review*, the typical Mexican migrant is a working-age male, between the ages of 18 and 35. According to the study's authors—Jorge Durand, Douglas S. Massey, and René M. Zenteno—Mexico's three western states of Guanajuato, Jalisco, and Michoacán have consistently provided a major portion of Mexican immigrants to the United States.

According to the study, the proportion of Mexican men and women immigrating to the United States from 1970 through 1994 remained consistent, at 75 percent male and 25 percent female. However, this analysis was based on statistics from 1994 and the years before. Studies of Mexican migration during the latter part of the 1990s have indicated an increase in the numbers of women and children migrating north.

A Dream of Prosperity

Despite improvements in its economy, Mexico continues to suffer from underemployment. As of early 2003, hundreds of thousands of southern Mexico's rural workers had indeed lost jobs because of NAFTA. Farmers could not compete against the lower-priced poultry and other agricultural products being shipped from the north. Major underemployment and wide-spread poverty in southern Mexico is considered a major factor behind undocumented immigrants deciding to enter the United States.

For legal immigrants as well as undocumented immigrants, the dream of earning enough money to improve their lives remains the main reason to leave Mexico. Greater economic opportunities lie in the prosperity of the north, where the wage rate is approximately 10 times that in Mexico. The journey is

An aerial view of Guanajuato City, the capital of Guanajuato. Along with two other western states, Jalisco and Michoacán, Guanajuato has consistently been a source of Mexican immigration to the United States.

regarded as an investment in the future. A story on immigration that appeared in the October 1998 issue of *National Geographic* describes the rationale behind one family's plans to send the father, Alejandro, to the United States. Alejandro had been caught a number of times trying to cross the border illegally before he finally made it into San Diego County:

> The family had planned the trip seriously. In Mexico, Alejandro had been making 600 pesos a month (about $70) as a car mechanic; from that and with loans from relatives they had saved the equivalent of almost a thousand dollars, some to pay for his bus fare and a fee to a *pollero*—a guide to get him across the border—and some to keep Lourdes going until the dollars Alejandro made started to flow south.
>
> The long-term goal was to save enough money so they could open a small business, probably a car repair shop, in Mexico City.
>
> "That is our dream," Lourdes said. "To tell the truth, if he were just working here that dream could not come true. Never."

3 IMMIGRATION TO THE NORTH

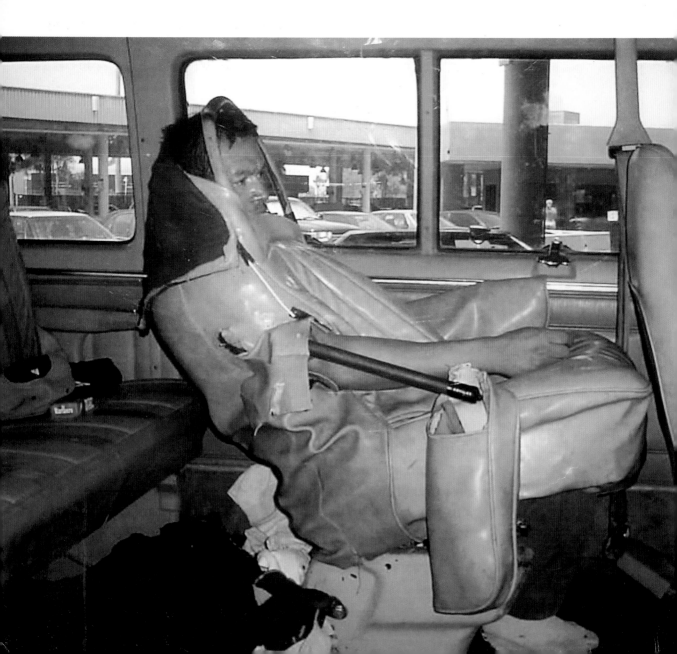

Mexican immigration to *El norte*, "the North," was not regulated until well into the 20th century. To place Mexican immigration in context, it is useful to briefly examine the history of U.S. and Canadian immigration.

Immigration to the United States has been characterized by openness punctuated by periods of restriction. During the 17th, 18th, and 19th centuries, immigration was essentially open without restriction, and, at times, immigrants were even recruited to come to America. Between 1783 and 1820, approximately 250,000 immigrants arrived at U.S. shores. Between 1841 and 1860, more than 4 million immigrants came; most were from England, Ireland, and Germany.

Historically, race and ethnicity have played a role in legislation to restrict immigration. The Chinese Exclusion Act of 1882, which was not repealed until 1943, specifically prevented Chinese people from becoming U.S. citizens and did not allow Chinese laborers to immigrate for the next decade. An agreement with Japan in the early 1900s prevented most Japanese immigration to the United States.

Until the 1920s, no numerical restrictions on immigration existed in the United States, although health restrictions applied. The only other significant restrictions came in 1917, when a reading or literacy test became a requirement for immigration (three U.S. presidents Cleveland, Taft, and Wilson had vetoed similar measures earlier). In addition, in 1917 a prohibition was

◄ Some individuals will go to great lengths to live and work in the United States; in this case a Mexican man has sewn himself in the back seat of a van in an attempt to evade border officials. The U.S. Bureau of Customs and Border Protection (BCBP), a branch of the newly formed Department of Homeland Security, is responsible for preventing and uncovering such attempts to unlawfully enter the country.

added to the law against the immigration of people from Asia (defined as the Asiatic barred zone). While a few of these prohibitions were lifted during World War II, they were not repealed until 1952, and even then Asians were only allowed in under very small annual quotas.

U.S. Immigration Policy from World War I to 1965

During World War I, the federal government required that all travelers to the United States obtain a visa at a U.S. consulate or diplomatic post abroad. As former State Department consular affairs officer C. D. Scully points out, by making that requirement permanent Congress, by 1924, established the framework of temporary, or non-immigrant visas (for study, work, or travel), and immigrant visas (for permanent residence). That framework remains in place today.

After World War I, cultural intolerance and bizarre racial theories led to new immigration restrictions. The House Judiciary Committee employed a eugenics consultant, Dr. Harry N. Laughlin, who asserted that certain races were inferior. Another leader of the eugenics movement, Madison Grant, argued that Jews, Italians, and others were inferior because of their supposedly different skull size.

The Immigration Act of 1924, preceded by the Temporary Quota Act of 1921, set new numerical limits on immigration based on "national origin." Taking effect in 1929, the 1924 act set annual quotas on immigrants that were specifically designed to keep out southern Europeans, such as Italians and Greeks. Generally no more than 100 people of the proscribed nationalities were permitted to immigrate.

While the new law was rigid, the U.S. Department of State's restrictive interpretation directed consular officers overseas to be even stricter in their application of the "public charge" provision. (A public charge is someone unable to support himself or his family.) As author Laura Fermi wrote, "In response to the new cry for restriction at the beginning of the [Great

Depression] . . . the consuls were to interpret very strictly the clause prohibiting admission of aliens 'likely to become public charges; and to deny the visa to an applicant who in their opinion might become a public charge at any time.'"

In the early 1900s, more than one million immigrants a year came to the United States. In 1930—the first year of the national-origin quotas—approximately 241,700 immigrants were admitted. But under the State Department's strict interpretations, only 23,068 immigrants entered during 1933, the smallest total since 1831. Later these restrictions prevented many Jews in Germany and elsewhere in Europe from escaping what would become the Holocaust. At the height of the Holocaust in 1943, the United States admitted fewer than 6,000 refugees.

The Displaced Persons Act of 1948, the nation's first refugee law, allowed many refugees from World War II to settle in the United States. The law put into place policy changes that had already seen immigration rise from 38,119 in 1945 to 108,721 in 1946 (and later to 249,187 in 1950). One-third of those admitted between 1948 and 1951 were Poles, with ethnic Germans forming the second-largest group.

The 1952 Immigration and Nationality Act is best known for its restrictions against those who supported communism or anarchy. However, the bill's other provisions were quite restrictive and were passed over the veto of President Truman. The 1952 act retained the national-origin quota system for the Eastern Hemisphere. The Western Hemisphere continued to operate without a quota and relied on other qualitative factors to limit immigration. Moreover, during that time, the Mexican bracero program, from 1942 to 1964, allowed millions of Mexican agricultural workers to work temporarily in the United States.

The 1952 act set aside half of each national quota to be divided among three preference categories for relatives of U.S. citizens and permanent residents. The other half went to aliens with high education or exceptional abilities. These quotas applied only to those from the Eastern Hemisphere.

One of the most pivotal immigration acts of the last 50 years was the 1965 Immigration and Nationality Act, signed by President Lyndon Johnson. Along with providing immigration opportunities to thousands of East Asians, the act gave greater priority to Mexican and other Latino immigrants with family sponsors.

A Halt to the National-Origin Quotas

The Immigration and Nationality Act of 1965 became a landmark in immigration legislation by specifically striking the racially based national-origin quotas. It removed the barriers to Asian immigration, which later led to opportunities to immigrate for many Filipinos, Chinese, Koreans, and others. The Western Hemisphere was designated a ceiling of 120,000 immigrants but without a preference system or per country limits. Modifications made in 1978 ultimately combined the Western and Eastern Hemispheres into one preference system and one ceiling of 290,000.

The 1965 act built on the existing system—without the national-origin quotas—and gave somewhat more priority to family relationships. It did not completely overturn the existing system but rather carried forward essentially intact the family immigration categories from the 1959 amendments to the

Immigration and Nationality Act. Even though the text of the law prior to 1965 indicated that half of the immigration slots were reserved for skilled employment immigration, in practice, Immigration and Naturalization Service (INS) statistics show that 86 percent of the visas issued between 1952 and 1965 went for family immigration.

A number of significant pieces of legislation since 1980 have shaped the current U.S. immigration system. First, the Refugee Act of 1980 removed refugees from the annual world limit and established that the president would set the number of refugees who could be admitted each year after consultations with Congress.

Second, the 1986 Immigration Reform and Control Act (IRCA) introduced sanctions against employers who "knowingly" hired undocumented immigrants (those here illegally). It also provided amnesty for many undocumented immigrants.

Third, the Immigration Act of 1990 increased legal immigration by 40 percent. In particular, the act significantly increased the number of employment-based immigrants (to 140,000), while also boosting family immigration.

Fourth, the 1996 Illegal Immigration Reform and Immigrant Responsibility Act (IIRAIRA) significantly tightened rules that permitted undocumented immigrants to convert to legal status and made other changes that tightened immigration law in areas such as political asylum and deportation.

Fifth, in response to the September 11, 2001, terrorist attacks, the USA PATRIOT Act and the Enhanced Border Security and Visa Entry Reform Act tightened rules on the granting of visas to individuals from certain countries and enhanced the federal government's monitoring and detention authority over foreign nationals in the United States.

New U.S. Immigration Agencies

In a dramatic reorganization of the federal government, the Homeland Security Act of 2002 abolished the Immigration and Naturalization Service and transferred its immigration service and enforcement functions from the Department of Justice into a new Department of Homeland Security. The Customs Service, the Coast Guard, and parts of other agencies were also transferred into the new department.

The Department of Homeland Security, with regards to immigration, is organized as follows: The Bureau of Customs and Border Protection (BCBP) contains Customs and Immigration inspectors, who check the documents of travelers to the United States at air, sea, and land ports of entry; and Border Patrol agents, the uniformed agents who seek to prevent unlawful entry along the southern and northern border. The new Bureau of Immigration and Customs Enforcement (BICE) employs

Mexican immigration to the United States has been strong and steady for several decades. By the 1990s, Mexicans had accounted for approximately 20 percent of all immigrants legally entering the country.

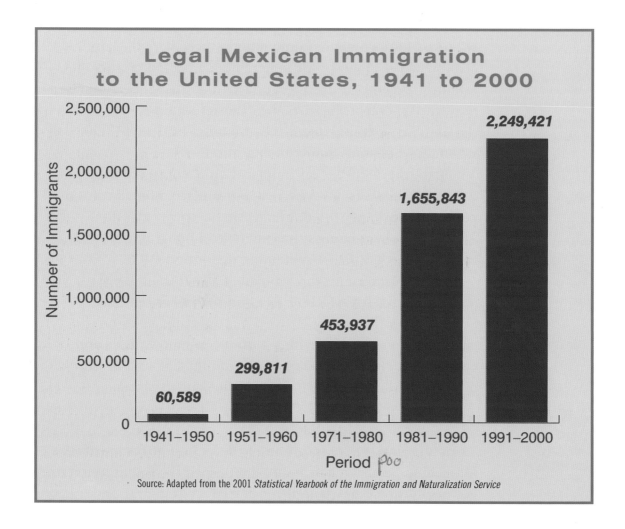

Legal Mexican Immigration to the United States, 1941 to 2000

Source: Adapted from the 2001 *Statistical Yearbook of the Immigration and Naturalization Service*

investigators, who attempt to find undocumented immigrants inside the United States, and Detention and Removal officers, who detain and seek to deport such individuals. The new Bureau of Citizenship and Immigration Services (BCIS) is where people go, or correspond with, to become U.S. citizens or obtain permission to work or extend their stay in the United States.

Following the terrorist attacks of September 11, 2001, the Department of Justice adopted several measures that did not require new legislation to be passed by Congress. Some of these measures created controversy and raised concerns about civil liberties. For example, FBI and INS agents detained for months more than 1,000 foreign nationals of Middle Eastern descent and refused to release the names of the individuals. It is alleged that the Department of Justice adopted tactics that discouraged the detainees from obtaining legal assistance. The Department of Justice also began requiring foreign nationals from primarily Muslim nations to be fingerprinted and questioned by immigration officers upon entry or if they have been living in the United States. Those involved in the September 11 attacks were not immigrants—people who become permanent residents with a right to stay in the United States—but holders of temporary visas, primarily visitor or tourist visas.

Today, the annual rate of legal immigration is lower than that at earlier periods in U.S. history. For example, from 1901 to 1910 approximately 10.4 immigrants per 1,000 U.S. residents came to the United States. Today, the annual rate is about 3.5 immigrants per 1,000 U.S. residents. While the percentage of foreign-born people in the U.S. population has risen above 11 percent, it remains lower than the 13 percent or higher that prevailed in the country from 1860 to 1930. Still, as has been the case previously in U.S. history, some people argue that even legal immigration should be lowered. These people maintain that immigrants take jobs native-born Americans could fill and that U.S. population growth, which immigration contributes to, harms the environment. In 1996 Congress voted against efforts to reduce legal immigration.

Most immigrants (800,000 to one million annually) enter the United States legally. But over the years the undocumented (illegal) portion of the population has increased to about 2.8 percent of the U.S. population—approximately 8 million people in all.

Today, the legal immigration system in the United States contains many rules, permitting only individuals who fit into certain categories to immigrate—and in many cases only after waiting anywhere from 1 to 10 years or more, depending on the demand in that category. The system, representing a compromise among family, employment, and human rights concerns, has the following elements:

> A U.S. citizen may sponsor for immigration a spouse, parent, sibling, or minor or adult child.

> A lawful permanent resident (green card holder) may sponsor only a spouse or child.

> A foreign national may immigrate if he or she gains an employer sponsor.

> An individual who can show that he or she has a "well-founded fear of persecution" may come to the country as a refugee—or be allowed to stay as an asylee (someone who receives asylum).

Beyond these categories, essentially the only other way to immigrate is to apply for and receive one of the "diversity" visas, which are granted annually by lottery to those from "underrepresented" countries.

In 1996 changes to the law prohibited nearly all incoming immigrants from being eligible for federal public benefits, such as welfare, during their first five years in the country. Refugees were mostly excluded from these changes. In addition, families who sponsor relatives must sign an affidavit of support showing they can financially take care of an immigrant who falls on hard times.

A Short History of Canadian Immigration

In the 1800s, immigration into Canada was largely unrestricted. Farmers and artisans from England and Ireland made up a significant portion of 19th-century immigrants. England's Parliament passed laws that facilitated and encouraged the voyage to North America, particularly for the poor.

After the United States barred Chinese railroad workers from settling in the country, Canada encouraged the immigration of Chinese laborers to assist in the building of Canadian railways. Responding to the racial views of the time, the Canadian Parliament began charging a "head tax" for Chinese and South Asian (Indian) immigrants in 1885. The fee of $50—later raised to $500—was well beyond the means of laborers making one or two dollars a day. Later, the government sought additional ways to prohibit Asians from entering the country. For example, it decided to require a "continuous journey," meaning that immigrants to Canada had to travel from their country on a boat that made an uninterrupted passage. For immigrants or asylum seekers from Asia this was nearly impossible.

As the 20th century progressed, concerns about race led to further restrictions on immigration to Canada. These restrictions particularly hurt Jewish and other refugees seeking to flee persecution in Europe. Government statistics indicate that Canada accepted no more than 5,000 Jewish refugees before and during the Holocaust.

After World War II, Canada, like the United States, began accepting thousands of Europeans displaced by the war. Canada's laws were modified to accept these war refugees, as well as Hungarians fleeing Communist authorities after the crushing of the 1956 Hungarian Revolution.

The Immigration Act of 1952 in Canada allowed for a "tap on, tap off" approach to immigration, granting administrative authorities the power to allow more immigrants into the country in good economic times, and fewer in times of recession. The shortcoming of such an approach is that there is little evidence immigrants harm a national economy and much evidence they contribute to economic growth, particularly in the growth of the labor force.

In 1966 the government of Prime Minister Lester Pearson

introduced a policy statement stressing how immigrants were key to Canada's economic growth. With Canada's relatively small population base, it became clear that in the absence of newcomers, the country would not be able to grow. The policy was introduced four years after Parliament enacted important legislation that eliminated Canada's own version of racially based national-origin quotas.

In 1967 a new law established a points system that awarded entry to potential immigrants using criteria based primarily on an individual's age, language ability, skills, education, family relationships, and job prospects. The total points needed for entry of an immigrant is set by the Minister of Citizenship and Immigration Canada. The new law also established a category for humanitarian (refugee) entry.

The 1976 Immigration Act refined and expanded the possibility for entry under the points system, particularly for those seeking to sponsor family members. The act also expanded refugee and asylum law to comport with Canada's international obligations. The law established five basic categories for immigration into Canada: 1) family; 2) humanitarian; 3) independents (including skilled workers), who immigrate to Canada on their own; 4) assisted relatives; and 5) business immigrants (including investors, entrepreneurs, and the self-employed).

The new Immigration and Refugee Protection Act, which took effect June 28, 2002, made a series of modifications to existing Canadian immigration law. The act, and the regulations that followed, toughened rules on those seeking asylum and the process for removing people unlawfully in Canada.

The law modified the points system, adding greater flexibility for skilled immigrants and temporary workers to become permanent residents, and evaluating skilled workers on the weight of their transferable skills as well as those of their specific occupation. The legislation also made it easier for employers to have a labor shortage declared in an industry or sector, which would facilitate the entry of foreign workers in that industry or sector.

On family immigration, the act permitted parents to sponsor dependent children up to the age of 22 (previously 19 was the maximum age at which a child could be sponsored for immigration). The act also allowed partners in common-law arrangements, including same-sex partners, to be considered as family members for the purpose of immigration sponsorship. Along with these liberalizing measures, the act also included

To the Other Side

Each day the INS makes hundreds of border apprehensions—arrests of immigrants as they attempt to cross the southern border without authorization. In an October 1998 story for *National Geographic* magazine, writer Michael Parfit described the typical day of a border agent as he observed him patrol outside Calexico, California:

> Luis Diaz, a U.S. Border Patrol watch commander, and I had found the bodies with the help of another agent, named Peter, who had a big night-vision scope mounted in the back of a pickup. By two-way radio he had guided Diaz and me across the field. "More to the east. Now south." Suddenly there the bodies were, lying facedown, looking like packages of hay wrapped in colored cloth, so much more still than they ought to be in the chilly damp moonlight of a California February night.

> "Make a line!" Diaz said to the bodies in Spanish. (Border agents here seem to call all illegals "bodies," as in, "There's two bodies moving toward area five.")

> "Hands on your heads!" Diaz went on. "Over to the car!" The bodies . . . got up, brushed off dirt and leaves, and started walking.

> "How did you see us?" one of them asked in Spanish. Diaz didn't answer. . . .

> "Where're you going?" Diaz asked them.

> "*Al otro lado*," one said.

> "*Sí*," said Diaz, "but where on the other side?"

> "Don't know," said one. "Los Angeles?"

> "It is beautiful, Los Angeles?" said another.

> "Well," said Diaz, "it's big."

> People from Central and South America call the United States *El norte*, but to many Mexicans it is just over there, the other side. It sounds mystical. In a way, for Mexicans buried in poverty, it is.

provisions to address perceived gaps in immigration-law enforcement.

Mexican Migration

During the first half of the 20th century, Mexican immigrants passed through a fairly open border. Illegal migration was not a major issue, most likely because the majority of Mexicans did not stay long in the United States. They traveled to jobs as seasonal workers and then returned home.

Many Mexican workers entered legally during the 1950s and 1960s as *braceros*, who provided a temporary labor force for growers based in the Southwest. During the period of the *bracero* program (1942–64), about 4.6 million Mexican migrant laborers legally entered the country, and then returned home after their seasonal work was done.

In the mid-1950s, the INS responded to complaints about illegal immigration by launching deportation programs such as Operation Wetback (*wetback* is an ethnic slur for the illegal Mexican immigrant; the term refers to how the immigrant

Mexican immigrants typically cross the border from one Mexican town to its sister city on the U.S. side. There are several sister towns between the 2,000-mile border stretching from California to Texas.

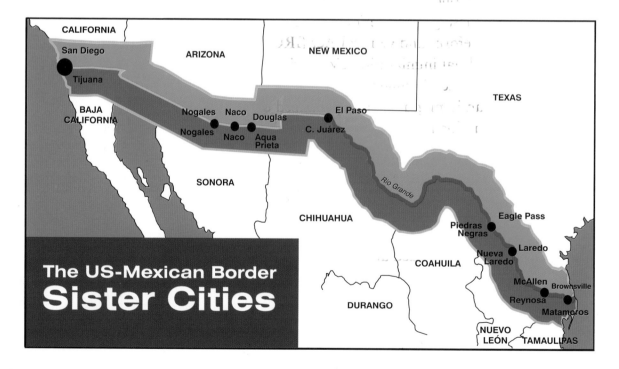

The US-Mexican Border
Sister Cities

crosses the border by swimming or wading at the Rio Grande).
This controversial operation led to the roundup and repatriation
of Mexicans to Mexico. Between 1954 and 1957 about 3.8 million Mexican immigrants and family members, some of whom
were citizens (having been born in the United States), were
rounded up from the Southwest and deported. The complaints
from American citizens, many of whom were of Mexican
American descent, that Operation Wetback was discriminatory
helped force the eventual termination of the operation.

During the 1960s, the number of legal Mexican immigrants
to the United States totaled about 430,000 (about 30,000 per
year). The following decade that figure grew to more than
680,000 (40,000 and more per year). From the 1960s to the
1980s the numbers of undocumented Mexican immigrants
entering the country rose steadily.

The Impact of the 1986 Immigration Reform and Control Act (IRCA) on Mexican Immigrants

Concerns about illegal immigration led in 1986 to Congress
passing, and President Ronald Reagan signing, the Immigration
Reform and Control Act (IRCA)—a law that sought to reduce
illegal immigration by making it more difficult for undocumented immigrants to obtain employment. For the first time,
an immigration law penalized employers who knowingly hired
undocumented workers. Employers were required to check the
personal documents—passports, driver's licenses, or birth
certificates—of potential employees that indicate legal status.
Employers who did not comply with the IRCA were subject to
fines and prison sentences.

While authorizing more resources for law enforcement, the act
also included an amnesty program for immigrants, pardoning
certain groups of undocumented immigrants living in the United
States and enabling them to obtain legal status. Amnesty was
available to those who had lived in the United States since
January 1, 1982, and agricultural laborers who worked at least

90 days between May 1, 1985, and May 1, 1986.

More than 3 million undocumented immigrants, including approximately 2 million Mexicans, took advantage of the program before it ended in May 1988. Many other Mexican immigrants who were eligible did not apply for amnesty, either because they did not know about the amnesty, lacked proof of residency (such as rental receipts) or employment (such as pay-check stubs), or received improper advice. Under the Legal Immigration Family Equity (LIFE) Act passed by Congress in 2000, tens of thousands of individuals who filed a class-action suit claiming the Immigration and Naturalization Service improperly advised them of their eligibility for the amnesty were given a chance to have their cases decided on an individual basis, with most expecting to receive approval.

In the years following the passage of IRCA, legal immigration from Mexico increased, in part because once granted legal status, formerly illegal Mexican immigrants had the right to petition for their spouses and children to join them. However, the 1986 legislation did not establish new or sufficient mechanisms for Mexicans to come into the United States and work temporarily with a legal status. The relative absence of legal

In 1986, U.S. President Ronald Reagan signed the Immigration Reform and Control Act, which tightened restrictions on employers of undocumented Mexican immigrants and gave amnesty to certain undocumented immigrant groups, including those living in the U.S. before 1982.

temporary visas for full-time work, combined with the continuing economic problems in Mexico and the demand for labor in the United States, led to additional undocumented workers coming to America from Mexico.

Over the next decade, the INS continued to apprehend and remove from the country millions of Mexicans seeking to enter the United States along the southern border. INS raids on factories on farms became controversial and were used less often as a means of immigration enforcement.

In 1994, concerns about undocumented immigrants using social services led to the presentation of Proposition 187 to California voters. This state statute was designed to prevent undocumented immigrants from receiving state benefits and services such as nonemergency medical care and public education. Republican governor Pete Wilson, who was running for reelection, made Proposition 187 and its anti-immigrant message a major part of his campaign platform. One of his ads showed Mexicans illegally crossing the border with a voiceover warning: "They just keep coming." The measure passed, carrying 60 percent of the vote. It was later struck down by federal judges as unconstitutional. Although the measure may have helped Pete Wilson be reelected as governor, Proposition 187 is widely viewed as having hurt the reputation of the Republican Party in California (and perhaps elsewhere) among the growing bloc of Hispanic voters.

Policing the Border

In recent years, Congress has funded a significant increase in additional law enforcement along the U.S.–Mexico border, also referred to as *La frontera*. Billions of dollars have been spent and thousands of Border Patrol Agents have been hired. At the 43 regular ports of entry, security cameras have monitored activity since their installation in the 1990s. A linked camera system operates 24 hours a day, digitally recording regular operations along the border.

Also, chain-link fences divide cities and scrubland. Thousands

of federal agents patrol the border in trucks and helicopters, on horseback and quad bikes to prevent illegal crossings. In desert areas they may drag car tires to smooth the sand, making it easier to spot footprints. In other areas seismic sensors buried under roads or along well-traveled paths detect the sound of footsteps. Floodlights illuminate fences, and infrared cameras track movements of anyone trying to slip across the border in the darkness.

While unlawful border crossings may receive a good deal of attention, more than 800,000 people travel back and forth across the U.S.–Mexican border through legal ports of entry every day. Whether walking or driving across, all must present their documents for inspection by the agents staffing the primary inspection booths at each port of entry. Those who drive often

Tijuana, Mexico, located just south of San Diego, California, was the busiest crossing point for immigrants during the 1980s and 1990s. Estimates indicated that half of all Mexican immigrants illegally entering the United States crossed into San Diego County during that period.

wait in long lines of traffic to present their documents at the inspections station and have their vehicle checked to ensure the driver is not smuggling goods or people.

Most Mexicans enter the United States from one of the Mexican border towns to its sister city on the U.S. side. These sister cities dot the 2,000-mile border, beginning at the Pacific in Tijuana, Mexico, and San Diego, California, and stretching to the Gulf of Mexico in Matamoros, Mexico, and Brownsville, Texas.

The booming industrial center of Tijuana draws thousands of workers to its many factories, but many do not stay long. During the 1980s and early 1990s, a 14-mile (22.5-km) stretch of the Tijuana-San Diego area was considered the busiest crossing point, especially for illegal immigration. Official estimates indicated that half of all immigrants illegally entering the United States crossed into San Diego County (downtown San Diego is 20 miles, or 32 km, north of the border).

East of San Diego lies Calexico, a small town across the border from the much larger city of Mexicali, Mexico, the state capital of Baja California. An important industrial center featuring a number of maquiladoras on its outskirts, Mexicali attracts millions of Mexicans in search of jobs, many of whom may later decide to try to cross the boundary fence to the United States, where the pay is better.

Further east in Arizona are four major border towns: Yuma, opposite San Luis, Mexico; Nogales, across from its Mexican namesake, Nogales; Naco, opposite Naco, Mexico (whose name comes from the last two letters of Arizona and Mexico); and Douglas, across from Agua Prieta, Mexico.

A 90-minute drive south of Tucson, Nogales is the busiest border-crossing station in Arizona and the second-largest point of entry for shipped produce. A July 2002 story for *Government Executive* entailed a description of the sophisticated camera system at the crossing in Nogales.

"The cameras provide daily security for our officers and backup in the case of a passenger complaint—we can pull the

A member of the human rights group Global Watch plants crosses in memory of the Mexicans who died trying to cross the U.S.–Mexico border. Some activists believe that immigration enforcement programs like Operation Hold the Line and Operation Gatekeeper resulted in more border-related deaths, as some immigrants risked taking routes over the border that were more dangerous.

video up right away and put that complaint to rest and protect the inspectors as well," said Joe Lafata, the port director in Nogales. "It's really a top-notch system. Many of the cameras have tilt-zoom capability. We can actually shoot into some of the hills here and watch the spotters [people paid by smugglers to spy on border-crossing operations] as they're watching us. They're there all the time and every once in a while you get a really nice portrait of them."

During the mid-1990s, Border Patrol enforcement efforts such as Operation Hold the Line and Operation Gatekeeper increased enforcement among traditional smuggling routes into Texas and California. Observers believe these programs encouraged smugglers to either attempt less-safe routes into those states or more entries through Arizona. With its easy access to the Pan American Highway, Douglas quickly became the largest entryway for undocumented immigrants. Its sister city, Agua Prieta, still caters to those looking to make desert crossings; city shops carry plastic water jugs, can openers, and other essential items for the desert traveler. Agua Prieta holds the distinction as the largest staging ground for illegal immigration.

Major towns found along Texas's long border with Mexico include El Paso, opposite Ciudad Juárez (the border's largest city), Mexico; Laredo, across from Nuevo Laredo; McAllen, across from Reynosa; and Brownsville, opposite Matamoros. More than 3 million trucks entered at the Laredo-Nuevo Laredo crossing in 2000, making it the busiest commercial crossing that year.

4 MAKING A NEW HOME

According to the 2000 U.S. Census, almost half of the Mexican-born population lives in two regions of the United States: the Los Angeles area and the state of Texas. In some Texan cities, such as El Paso, San Antonio, Corpus Christi, and Laredo, Hispanics (mostly of Mexican descent) have become the majority population. Mexicans comprise about 20 percent of the population of Texas.

However, over the years far more Mexican immigrants have chosen to settle in California. That state contains the most Mexican immigrants in the nation (about 43 percent of the total immigrant population). The biggest pocket of growth is in Los Angeles. As early as 1925 more people of Mexican descent lived in Los Angeles than in any Mexican city except Mexico City, the capital. The same is true today: the Los Angeles–Long Beach area has a Mexican population of about 900,000, a greater number of Mexicans than in any other city in the Western Hemisphere (again, with the exception of Mexico City).

More than three-fourths of Mexicans living in the United States reside in just four states: California, Texas, Illinois, and Arizona. Other states with significant Mexican-immigrant populations include Florida, Colorado, Nevada, New York, and North Carolina. However, with each passing year Mexican immigrants—both documented and undocumented—are making their homes in states across North America.

◀A busy street in a Mexican neighborhood, New York City. There are many predominantly Mexican neighborhoods in the United States, some that are still growing every year. The most established of these neighborhoods are in Los Angeles, Chicago, various Texan cities, and New York City, where the Mexican population tripled during the 1990s.

Southwestern cities with large Mexican American populations include San Diego, California; Tucson, Arizona; Albuquerque, New Mexico; Dallas, Texas; and San Antonio, Texas. But large Mexican American populations can also be found in New York, Chicago, Detroit, Denver, and Kansas City. In New York City, the Mexican population tripled during the 1990s, growing from 93,000 in 1990 to nearly 300,000, according to the 2000 Census. Even Vancouver, Canada, boasts its own "Little Mexico," a Mexican immigrant community located in the heart of the city.

This map illustrates the numbers of Mexican immigrants naturalized in U.S. states in 2001. The four leading states in this category were California, Texas, Illinois, and Arizona.

Mexican Immigrants Naturalized by State, Fiscal Year 2001

618
11
1
2
613
199
4
135
315
10
19
96
53
243
1,126
71
862
383
173
189
13
350
395
109
263
1,014
615
6,985
65
39
224
21
11
147
58,780
86
380
4,315
349
362
21
48
26
20
236
29
15,303
1,604
60
49

Source: Adapted from the 2001 *Statistical Yearbook of the Immigration and Naturalization Service*

A large family of Mexicans sits outside their home in Laredo, Texas. In some cases, the living conditions Mexican immigrants face in U.S. border cities are similar to what they faced in Mexico, but the promise of higher wages persuades them to remain in the United States.

The 1990s saw a trend in which many Mexican immigrants chose to move to small U.S. towns, rather than the big cities. They were following manufacturing or meat processing jobs that relocated from urban areas during the 1980s and 1990s. The small towns and rural areas prove appealing to new immigrants. Living expenses in these areas can be much lower than in barrios (a Spanish-speaking section of a city or town). Sometimes the environment is similar to that of the villages immigrants left in rural Mexico.

Hundreds of residents from just one village in Mexico have

been known to follow one another to the same town or neighborhood in the United States. In the *New York Times*, Kevin Sack described how this migration pattern affected the town of East Point, Georgia (population 40,000), during the 1990s. East Point became the destination for hundreds of Mexican immigrants from Ejido Modelo, a village located in the state of Jalisco, in western Mexico. Most found work as fabricators at an East Point plant, and lived near one another in a tight-knit barrio.

Some of these immigrants had lived in Georgia since 1984—and had taken advantage of the 1986 amnesty program that made them legal residents. Others were new arrivals; their presence had significantly affected the 2000 Census count, helping raise the Hispanic population of the town to 7.6 percent. According to Sack, similar Mexican migration has taken place in

A Mexican migrant worker harvests tobacco on a farm in Kentucky. Since the early 20th century, the numbers of Mexican farmworkers in the United States have been decreasing, though they still make up a large segment of the country's agricultural labor force.

Sharing the Paycheck with Family Back Home

Over the years, Mexican citizens working in the United States have channeled billions of their hard-earned dollars into Mexico's economy. Many Mexican immigrants regularly send part of each paycheck home to family members. Such transactions are called remittances. During the 1990s, Mexican immigrants supplemented their relatives' incomes by more than $4.5 billion.

The cash continued to flow at an even greater rate with the new millennium. In the year 2000 Mexican immigrants sent home $6 billion (about $17 million a day). And according to an April 2002 study by Mexico's National Population Council, an agency of the Ministry of the Interior, Mexican families received a record $8.9 billion dollars in 2001. "On average, receiving households obtained about $3,000 a year—$2,000 in rural households and a little less than $4,000 in urban homes," the council noted. "That equaled a little less than 40 percent of total income."

These financial contributions of Mexican immigrants in the United States to family members back home have become Mexico's third-largest source of revenue, surpassed only by oil and tourism.

small towns throughout the south, where it has "created large pockets of Latino culture where there had once been none."

Getting a Job

During the latter part of the 1800s and well into the 1900s, many Mexicans crossed the border to work temporary agricultural jobs as migrant laborers. They traveled to farms or orchards, where they harvested crops, then returned home at the end of the growing season. Migrant workers picked cotton in Texas or harvested grapes on large farm estates in California's Central Valley. The work was hard and low-paying, but still provided more income than was possible to earn in Mexico. As the U.S. economy became industrialized, workers also found jobs with railroad and mining companies.

Early migrant workers found jobs by paying a labor agent to connect them with farms or ranches in need of workers.

A Mexican cook at a restaurant in Austin, Texas, presents a serving of tamales. Since the 1970s, a growing segment of the Mexican workforce has been landing jobs in U.S. cities.

However, during the 1970s, as more and more Mexican immigrants found jobs that weren't in the agricultural sector, new immigrants came to depend more on friends and families for job advice. Because most of these jobs were in service and manufacturing industries, which are located in or near urban areas, more Mexicans gravitated to the cities where friends and families had already settled. By the early 1990s, most Mexicans lived in or near a city. Only a portion of Mexicans works in agriculture today; however, Mexican immigrants still make up a large proportion of the farmworker labor force in the United States.

Other Support

Several Mexican American organizations offer information, programs, and various kinds of assistance to Mexican immigrants, including the Mexican American Legal Defense and Educational Fund (MALDEF), the National Council of *La Raza*, and the American GI Forum, which was founded by Dr. Hector P. García after World War II. García was inspired to start the Forum, which has approximately 50,000 members today, after a Texas funeral home refused to rebury Félix Longoria, a decorated WWII veteran, because he was Mexican.

One of the earliest groups, the League of United Latin

American Citizens (LULAC), was founded in 1929. LULAC grew in large part out of a response to the discrimination that Mexican Americans faced at the time. During the 1920s, throughout much of the Southwest region Mexicans met with the same "whites only" segregation that African Americans were suffering in the South. Restaurant owners would refuse to serve Mexican customers. Stores and cinemas posted signs that announced, "No Mexicans allowed." Mexican children had to attend segregated schools; they and their families were excluded from facilities such as parks, swimming pools, and public buses and trains.

Concerned Mexican Americans organized and fought back through LULAC. The organization filed lawsuits to end segregation in public facilities, lobbied for Mexican American rights, and provided legal assistance to Mexican Americans who had been arrested. In the 1940s, LULAC successfully took legal action against California and Texas school districts to eliminate the segregation of Mexican students.

Getting a Green Card

Non-U.S. citizens who are eligible can apply for a green card, which grants them permission to live and work indefinitely in the country, although the process of getting the card can take several years. Officially called the Alien Registration Receipt Card Form I-151, the green card was first issued in the 1940s, when it was actually green. In the years that followed, many designs of the card appeared, most often in various shades of blue. With the green card, which is valid indefinitely (unless its owner leaves the United States for more than a year or is jobless for more than six months), foreign residents can live and work anywhere in the United States.

5 CHOOSING BETWEEN THE OLD AND THE NEW

Close-knit Mexican communities in the United States have continuously provided a warm welcome for Mexican immigrants, allowing them to hold on to parts of their culture as they have adjusted to a foreign culture and language. Immigrants still often name their neighborhoods after the village they came from, or simply refer to the area as "Little Mexico." Newcomers can feel comfortable in these neighborhoods, knowing they can easily communicate with others who live there.

Long-established Mexican neighborhoods, such as East Los Angeles, East San Jose, and South El Paso, which have existed for many decades, provide a comfortable environment for the newcomer. Businesses offer the same items purchased south of the border. Grocery stores supply tortillas, mole (a spicy sauce), salsa *chipotl*, and other Mexican foods. Local pharmacies offer medicines from Mexico, including medicinal teas, herbs, and ointments. In hundreds of Mexican neighborhoods, buildings display colorful murals—originally inspired by Mexican artist Diego Rivera—that proclaim pride in Mexico's history and heritage.

At home, the Spanish-speaking immigrant can watch a variety of television programs in his or her own language. The two largest Spanish-language channels, Univision and Telemundo, offer *telenovelas* (soap operas), game shows, dubbed versions

◀ A furniture store in a Hispanic neighborhood of Santa Ana, California, advertises for a Valentine's Day sale in Spanish. In this and other Hispanic neighborhoods in U.S. cities, Mexican restaurants, grocery stores, and convenience stores serve as reminders to Mexican newcomers of their homeland.

of American programs, and well as coverage of the ever popular sport of *fútbol* (soccer).

Importance of Family

Family ties are strong in Mexican culture, whether in the home country or an American barrio. Most Mexican immigrants teach their children the value of working for the good of the whole family, not just the individual. These strong ties extend to grandparents, aunts, uncles, and cousins as well. Family members help each other whenever possible, financially and emotionally.

Mexican immigrants often socialize with other immigrant families, many of whom came from the same village or region of Mexico. With family and friends they preserve cherished traditions and rituals in celebrating major life events, such as baptisms, weddings, and funerals. Such gatherings and celebrations often feature traditional dishes originating from the family's home in Mexico. Musical entertainment might include singing of *corridos* (folk ballads) or performances of mariachi bands (groups playing violins, guitars, and trumpets).

Mexicans also observe family anniversaries such as birthdays with traditional food and drink. A special tradition that highlights children's parties is the breaking of the piñata, a *papier mâché* or clay pot in the shape of a person or animal that is filled with candy. The piñata is hung from rope, and blindfolded children take turns trying to strike it with a stick and break it open—releasing its delicious contents to the delight of partygoers. A popular party staple for many generations in Mexico, piñatas can be found for sale in retail and party stores across America. Families with and without Mexican heritage traditionally include piñatas in birthday celebrations.

A girl's 15th birthday celebration receives special attention in many Mexican households. The *quinceañera* is a ceremony that can be as elaborate as a wedding, complete with fancy dresses,

Painter Diego Rivera (1886–1957) was a leading figure of the Mexican mural movement of the 1920s. His work was a source of national pride for Mexicans, and inspired the many Mexican-themed murals that can be found in U.S. cities today.

a sit-down meal, a hired photographer, and traditional or contemporary Mexican and American music. The religious ceremony of the *quinceañera* takes place in the Catholic Church in a special mass. At that time the girl being honored renews her vow of commitment to the Church. Afterwards, everyone celebrates with a party. Sometimes the *quinceañera* takes place in the girl's home. She may be serenaded by a mariachi band's performance of the folk song "Las Mañanitas."

National and Religious Celebrations

Community celebrations also revolve around Mexico's national holidays. Most Mexican Americans feel an intense loyalty to Mexico, and celebrate its two major national holidays: Independence Day and Cinco de Mayo.

Independence Day, observed on September 16, commemorates the date in 1821 that Father Miguel Hidalgo delivered a speech proclaiming the end of Spanish colonial rule. On Cinco de Mayo (the fifth of May) Mexicans celebrate the anniversary of General Benito Juárez's victory over France's superior military force, in 1862, at the Battle of Puebla. Mexicans across the

Mariachi bands are common to most Mexican secular and religious holidays, particularly the *quinceañera*, which celebrates a Mexican girl's 15th birthday.

country celebrate both of these holidays with fiestas, parades, folk dancing, and music, as well as speeches by public figures.

Many Mexicans are deeply religious. In their new country Mexican immigrants continue to observe the traditions, ceremonies, and festivals of their strong Roman Catholic faith, the majority religion in Mexico. Family baptisms, First Communions, confirmations, marriages, and funerals take place in the church, as well as observances of religious holidays such as Lent and Christmas. Many Catholic parishes located in Hispanic neighborhoods perform masses in Spanish and include traditional Mexican music.

Native American and African beliefs and practices play an important part in Mexican Catholicism, especially festivities

Independence Day and Cinco de Mayo (the fifth of May) are two popular festivals that are celebrated in Mexican American communities. (Above) A group of men in warrior costume salute with their swords during an Independence Day procession on September 16. The holiday commemorates the day in 1821 Mexico officially declared its freedom from Spanish colonial rule.

For Cinco de Mayo, revelers dress up in French and Mexican military uniforms to reenact the Battle of Puebla in 1862, in which General Benito Juárez led his troops to victory over the French.

celebrating patron saints. Of particular importance to Mexican immigrants across North America is December 12, celebrated as the Feast Day of Our Lady of Guadalupe. The holiday commemorates the appearance of the Virgin Mary to an Aztec Indian peasant, Juan Diego, in 1531. According to the legend, the Virgin filled Diego's cloak with red roses and left her image on the back of his garment. Many Mexicans consider the Virgin of Guadalupe as the patron saint of all Mexico, and the spiritual mother of oppressed people. The Basilica de Guadalupe in Mexico City was built on the site where the Virgin Mary is said to have appeared.

In Mexico, Catholics celebrate Antorcha Guadalupana, a tradition begun more than 50 years ago in which runners carry a torch from the Basilica de Guadalupe to their home parish or village, calculating their arrival for December 12, in time for the feast day. The Antorcha tradition is also followed in New York City, home to an estimated 300,000 Mexican immigrants. After a mass at St. Patrick's Cathedral, on Fifth Avenue, runners bear blazing torches through the streets to their local parishes. In

2002, organizers set up a 3,133-mile (5,042-km) torch relay that originated at the Basilica de Guadalupe in Mexico City and ended at St. Patrick's Cathedral in New York City.

The Feast Day of Our Lady of Guadalupe traditionally begins with an early morning mass during which churchgoers sing *mañanitas*, traditional songs of greeting to the Virgin. Others may carry red roses or images of the Virgin Mary. Afterwards fiestas with music and great food spill over to the blocks of Mexican neighborhoods.

This celebration takes on special significance for many

An Aztec Indian dance is performed in front of the Basilica of Our Lady of Guadalupe during the annual Feast Day. The Aztec performance helps practicing Mexicans remember Juan Diego, an Aztec who is said to have been visited by the Virgin Mary in 1531. Mexican communities hold similar celebrations in North America.

Dual Nationality

For years, Mexican immigrants who were naturalized as U.S. citizens forfeited their rights as citizens of Mexico. In 1998 the Mexican government changed this policy, effectively offering dual nationality to the more than 2 million Mexican-born immigrants who, in becoming U.S. citizens, had lost their status as Mexican nationals. When the law went into effect, hundreds of applicants flocked to their local Mexican consulates throughout the United States to apply for the new designation.

For a $12 fee, applicants received an official Declaration of Mexican Nationality, a document that gave its holder economic privileges such as the right to buy and sell property in Mexico (foreigners face certain restrictions) and apply for Mexican identity cards and passports.

The new status will ease travel restrictions for many Mexican immigrants when they want to travel home. Consuelo LaMonica explained to the *Hispanic Times Magazine*, "We share a deep emotional attachment to Mexico, even though we have been in this country for a long time. . . . Now, with my new dual nationality, I can go back and forth across the border to visit family without a problem."

Mexican immigrants living north of the border. One immigrant explained to the *New York Times* in December 1998: "All Mexicans are more united because we have a day to celebrate here. We are taking this day to tell more people and more people we want to live in the United States with all the rights everybody else has."

Besides meeting the spiritual needs of its parish members, the Catholic Church also provides for the physical well-being of many new immigrants by providing welfare services, referrals to housing authority agencies, and assistance with filling out forms.

About a third of American Catholics are Hispanic, most of them Mexican. The Catholic Church continues to reach out to the Mexican community, as in March 2002, when it announced plans to canonize Juan Diego, whose visions of the Virgin Mary over 500 years ago inspired many Mexican traditions centered around the sacred figure.

Joining American Society

Many scholars consider immigrants to be assimilated, or a part of American mainstream society, when they have obtained good English skills, financial security, and U.S. citizenship. By some of these standards, Mexicans have not had as high a rate of assimilation into the United States as some other immigrant groups. Geographic proximity is a main factor affecting those Mexican immigrants who do not pursue naturalization. In other words, those who expect that after a temporary stay they will take the opportunity to return home may choose not to become citizens. This is also true of many Canadian immigrants.

Yet in many cases Mexican immigrants end up remaining in their new home a long time, and still have limited success in assimilating. Columnist Linda Chavez noted in the magazine *American Enterprise* that a high percentage of new immigrants had limited language abilities: "As of 1990, three-quarters of

A Mexican man (left) is sworn in as a U.S. citizen during a mass naturalization ceremony in Miami, Florida.

Mexican immigrants who arrived in the 1980s still spoke little or no English." Immigrants who do not learn English have fewer job choices and typically receive low wages.

However, during the late 1990s Hispanic household income rose steadily for several years. And, according to Tamar Jacoby, who analyzed immigration studies in *American Enterprise*, some Hispanics do reach middle-class financial security. She reported that half of all Latinos owned their own homes within 20 years of arriving in the United States.

Some resourceful immigrants solve the low-wage predicament by taking on several jobs, eventually earning enough money to buy a car, furniture, and a home. Others rely on their experiences as low-wage workers in landscape, construction, or cleaning firms to set up similar businesses.

Becoming a Citizen

Immigrants who choose to become citizens of the United States must meet the following criteria: they must be at least 18 years old (minor children can receive citizenship through their parents) and have been a lawful permanent resident for at least five years, or three years if married to a U.S. citizen. In addition, they must be able to speak, read, and write the English language, be familiar with the government and history of the United States, and be of "good moral character." During the naturalization ceremony, participants must swear an oath of loyalty to the United States.

Immigrants to Canada who wish to be naturalized can retain the citizenship of their native country. Candidates for citizenship must be at least 18 years old (minor children can receive citizenship through their parents) and have lived as a legal resident in Canada for three of the previous four years. They must be able to understand and speak English or French well and have a basic knowledge of the history, government, and geography of Canada. The naturalization process involves applying to a citizenship court, appearing at a hearing before a citizenship examiner, and participating in a naturalization ceremony.

Second-Generation Mexicans

Often children of immigrants grow up straddling two worlds, talking with their parents in Spanish at home and speaking English at school. This next generation grows up bilingual—able to speak in two languages. They may act as interpreters, helping Spanish-speaking family members deal with educational, medical, or other issues outside their immediate community.

Most Mexican immigrants prefer that their children speak both Spanish and English. But about half of the children of Hispanic immigrants assimilate into the English-speaking community to such an extent that they don't learn to speak Spanish, or they speak it poorly.

As second-generation immigrants grow up speaking English, they tend to accept the values and ideas of the culture around them. Sometimes the children's new ideas and values clash with those of their parents. For instance, there are first-generation parents who do not approve of girls playing sports, a popular school activity in America. Children may rebel against adults, ignoring the traditional value of always showing respect to elders. Some extended generations of Mexican families have dropped their allegiance to Roman Catholicism, adopting Protestant faiths instead.

Mexican immigrants want to keep the traditional values of their culture, which at times seem at odds with those of the mainstream American culture. In a poll conducted by the Pew Hispanic Center and the Kaiser Family Foundation in 2002, more than 76 percent of Hispanics believed that their children would be better educated and make more money than they did. However, only 56 percent believed their children would hold the same moral values.

Mexico's Change in Attitude

When President Vicente Fox took office in 2000, one of his first acts was the creation of a special federal agency: the Office for Mexicans Living Abroad. The new department represented the interests of approximately 20 million legal and illegal Mexican immigrants living in the United States.

The official recognition given to Mexican immigrants reflected a change of heart for the Mexican government, which for years had looked down on immigrants who left to seek their fortune in America. They were considered traitors, a reminder that Mexico could not create enough work for its own people.

President Fox praised Mexican immigrants as "national heroes," and pointed out their "courage, determination, perseverance and valor," as evidenced by their accomplishments in America. Mexicans living in the United States reacted positively to the attention. The Office for Mexicans Living Abroad closed within two years, however, and its duties were absorbed by the Ministry of Foreign Relations and the Mexican consulates in the United States.

6 PROBLEMS FACING MEXICAN IMMIGRANTS

While legal Mexican immigrants face many difficulties in America, far greater problems await undocumented immigrants, many of whom risk their lives attempting to enter the country by crossing the border illegally.

Deadly Border Crossings

In October 2002 a worker at a grain storage facility in Denison, Oklahoma, discovered the badly decomposed bodies of 11 adults who had been locked inside a railcar. Four months earlier, the train had been in service in Matamoros, Mexico (across the border from Brownsville, Texas). After entering the United States, the hopper car sat for several months in a storage yard before the rail worker made his grisly discovery. It was not the first time that a railcar entombed would-be illegal immigrants. In July 1987, 18 Mexican men had been found dead inside a locked boxcar in Sierra Blanca, Texas.

Millions of Mexican immigrants have risked their lives trying to cross the border illegally. Some pay coyotes (smugglers) to guide them in darkness across the border or conceal them in vehicles traveling north. These coyotes recruit their customers, or *pollos* (literally, "chickens" in Spanish), at bus stops, public parks, plazas, and hotels in Mexican border towns, charging anywhere from $750 to more than $1,000 per person. Sometimes the coyote employs others: a *vendepollo* (chicken seller) to recruit clients, a *brincador* (fence jumper) to lead the

◀ An unmarked burial site in San Diego for unidentified Mexicans who died trying to illegally enter the U.S. Undocumented immigrants often rely on smugglers known as coyotes for help, though typically these profiteers have little concern for the immigrants' safety.

Migrant Deaths by Type, Fiscal Years 1999–2002

Type of Death	1999	2000	2001	2002
Exposure-Heat	59	144	123	137
Exposure-Cold	17	17	4	7
Train	17	5	3	2
Car Accident	22	48	27	28
Confined Space	1	0	0	2
Drowning	76	95	74	58
Unknown	41	47	97	77
Other	17	27	8	9
Total	250	383	336	320

Source: U.S. Border Patrol

migrants across the border, and a driver to deliver them to a safe house. After payment is made (often wired by a relative already living in the United States), the undocumented immigrant can leave for his or her final destination.

In the mid-1990s, when the INS beefed up the Border Patrol and increased security at crossing points in Texas and California, coyotes steered their clients into the less-patrolled desert areas, including those in Arizona. In Douglas, Arizona, much of the border was unfenced; beyond it was state and federal lands, Indian reservations, and property owned by ranchers.

Concerns about undocumented immigrants often focus on services they may receive from state and local governments. Since undocumented immigrants in border areas usually do not have health insurance, the costs of their health care can become absorbed by local public hospitals in border communities.

These types of concerns have led to calls for greater federal reimbursements and increased enforcement at the border. In response to the increase in migrant traffic, the Border Patrol boosted the number of its agents in the Douglas area from 58 in 1994 to 435 in 2000. In one month alone, agents in the area

In recent years, the U.S. Border Patrol has recorded the cause of death for migrants illegally crossing the U.S.–Mexico border. Between 2000 and 2002, heat exposure was the leading cause of death.

apprehended more than 70,000 immigrants as they attempted to cross the border.

Increased enforcement efforts have pushed smugglers to venture into even more isolated and dangerous areas. Although undocumented immigrants often depend on coyotes to guide them to safety, these smugglers have at times shown little concern for human life. Some smugglers have abandoned migrants without food or water in the desert, where some die of exhaustion or heat dehydration. Sometimes coyotes have led their charges to bandits, who attack and sometimes kill the hapless travelers.

Migrants who are transported by truck or van sometimes fare little better. Coyotes have been known to pack as many as 40 people, without food or water, into the back of a truck. As the vehicle heats up during the journey along desert roads, the occupants crammed inside its metal walls succumb to heat exhaustion. To pass safely through highway checkpoints, smugglers have been known to force immigrants from a truck, promising they will be met further down the highway. Then the truck may never show up at the designated meeting point, or, worse, the undocumented immigrants become lost in the desert.

Death and Disease

The rivers separating Mexico and the United States have proven deadly for some undocumented immigrants, who have drowned while trying to cross the Rio Grande to Texas or the All-American Canal to California.

Other undocumented immigrants suffer serious infections and disease resulting from wading through the sewage-filled New River, which flows north from Mexicali to the Salton Sea at the California border. A vast repository of agricultural and industrial waste, the river contains microbes that cause a variety of illnesses, ranging from hepatitis A to cholera. It is considered by some the most polluted river in the United States.

The Tijuana-San Diego crossing had been the border's most heavily trafficked crossing site before Operation Gatekeeper funneled traffic to the east in the mid-1990s. So many immigrant groups were crossing along Interstate 5 in San Diego that the state of California put up yellow caution signs. Each sign—which features the figures of a running man, woman, and child—indicates places on the freeway where drivers need to watch out for migrants who have just crossed the border. Despite the warning signs, hundreds of people have been struck and killed over the years.

The number of immigrants killed while attempting to enter the United States has risen, despite advertised warnings by the U.S. Border Patrol about the dangers of desert crossings (featured on posters and in Spanish-language radio spots in Mexico). In 2000 the Border Patrol recorded 383 deaths of undocumented immigrants along the border—an average of more than one per day. Over the next two years the number of deaths declined, though immigration authorities continued to address the problem of illegal crossings. The Border Patrol added a number of special teams that specialize in saving

A Mexican girl wades through the sewage-filled New River to cross the border into Calexico, California. By entering the river, immigrants risk exposing themselves to a number of infections and diseases.

migrants in difficult or life-threatening situations along the southern border areas. Border Patrol statistics indicate Border Patrol Agents and special teams have rescued hundreds of migrants every year.

Bilingual Education and ESL

During the mid-1900s, Latino advocates pushed to change public school systems, encouraging them to offer programs that would let Spanish-speaking children learn in their native language. As early as the 1930s and 1940s one educator, George Isidore Sanchez (1906–72), sought edu-

A sign warns motorists to watch out for immigrants crossing the highway. These signs have become a necessity in San Diego, where hundreds of immigrants have been struck and killed by cars.

cational reforms. One important reform in particular was the establishment of bilingual instruction for Spanish-speaking children. But it was not until the Chicano movement of the 1960s that some of his ideas about using Spanish-speaking teachers and studying the contributions of Mexican Americans were put into practice.

In 1968 Congress passed the Bilingual Education Act, which provided federal funds to public schools for programs taught in the Spanish language. School districts could use the money to hire bilingual teachers and materials for teaching children who

did not speak English as their first language.

Teachers of bilingual-education classes in Hispanic communities taught English-language skills while presenting curriculum content (such as math, science, social studies, and language arts) in Spanish. Later, students could transition into classes taught only in English. Another form of bilingual education brings together Spanish-speaking and English-speaking students, who together take some subjects in Spanish and others in English. This way each ethnic group learns the other's language.

Many schools rely on the English as a Second Language (ESL) program, in which Spanish-speaking and other foreign students attend one or more classes where they practice speaking and writing English or are taught curriculum subjects in their native tongue. For the rest of the school day, these students return to the mainstream, English-speaking classes.

Since the 1960s, bilingual education has remained controversial. Many school districts have complained about having to pay additional costs for bilingual programs, but a 1974 decision by the Supreme Court ruled that public schools had to

An English as a Second Language (ESL) class for adults, located in Los Angeles. Language instruction for younger Hispanic students has been a debated issue for years in the U.S.; school leaders clash the most over how and when Hispanic students should begin receiving instruction in English.

provide for students who did not speak English as their native language. In the 1980s the federal government cut funds for the program. Over the years several states, including Arizona and California, passed laws banning the program in public schools.

Education researchers disagree about the effectiveness of bilingual education. Supporters of the program claim it would be more effective if it was properly funded. Opponents of bilingual education say that children would readily learn English and that compelling children to learn in Spanish holds them back in a society where speaking English is a crucial job qualification.

The Matricula Consular

In March 2002, the Mexican government authorized its consulates to begin issuing an updated version of its *matricula consular*, an identity card that indicates the name and age of the holder. The U.S. government did not accept this form of ID, but many state and local organizations found it acceptable. By the end of 2002 more than 600 police departments, over 80 city and county governments, and thousands of businesses accepted the identity card. In 13 states, including North Carolina and Utah, the *matricula consular* was considered valid identification for a driver's license application. Immigrants in Texas could use the card to apply for in-state tuition at state universities.

Many banks accepted the new ID card, making it easier for undocumented immigrants to open accounts and transfer money back home. Previously immigrants had to send cash using international money transfer companies, such as Western Union or MoneyGram. Such businesses charged high fees or offered low exchange rates. In some cases, immigrants lost anywhere from 10 to 25 percent of the amount being sent. (The average check ranged from $200 to $300.)

However, with a bank or credit union account, the immigrant has a less expensive way to send money—transfer it electronically from the United States to Mexico. By the end of 2002 at least 60 major banks, including Bank of America, Wells Fargo, and Citibank, located mostly in Spanish-speaking communities, were accepting the consular identity card. In 2003, the fate of the *matricula consular* became uncertain as U.S. Congressional critics argued that the card contained few security features and, therefore, could be forged by someone seeking to obtain a new identity.

In 1998, California voters approved Proposition 227, an initiative that banned bilingual education in all the state's public schools and replaced it with an English immersion program, which required students speaking a foreign language to learn in an all-English environment. The measure was immediately challenged; however, in October 2002, the federal appeals court upheld the initiative, and the ban remained in place.

Returning Home

Unlike immigrants from Asia or Europe, Mexicans live near their homeland. The proximity of Mexico to the United States makes it relatively easy for Mexican Americans to return home. According to a study published in the *Latin American Research Review* in 2001, return migration to Mexico rose from 15 percent in 1970–74 to 25 percent in 1990–94. Some of those traveling south across the border may actually be commuters. A number of Mexicans who live near the border cross it on a daily basis, traveling to work in the United States and then returning to their homes in Mexico. In some border areas, such commuters make up about 16 percent of the workforce of U.S. border towns.

Once immigrants are granted the status of permanent residence, it becomes easier and less expensive to go back and forth between Mexico and the United States. Legalized immigrants return home to celebrate Christmas holidays, for summer visits, or special celebrations. For example, each January many of the Mexican and Mexican American families living in Detroit journey south for *Las fiestas patronales*, a 10-day period of festivals honoring the patron saints of Mexican villages.

Still others return home because the United States did not help them fulfill their dreams. According to a 1997 study

◀ The Mexican flag flies over the Palacio Nacional in Mexico City. Many Mexican immigrants travel back and forth between the United States and their homeland, and a significant portion of the immigrant population move back to Mexico for good, although in recent years fewer undocumented immigrants have returned for fear they will be apprehended by immigration officers.

reported by Belinda Reyes of the Public Policy Institute of California, based in San Francisco, half of all legal and undocumented Mexican immigrants returned home within two years. Only 20 percent stayed for more than five years. Some demographers dispute these findings, noting Reyes's study is based on data that may be outdated (1980s and early '90s).

As of 2000, fewer undocumented immigrants living in the United States chose to return to Mexico for visits to friends and family. As border enforcement increased during the late 1990s, so did the costs that smugglers demanded of their cus-

The backyard of an immigrant family's home in Laredo, Texas. Many Mexican families return home after their expecations of a better life in the United States go unfulfilled.

tomers. In a study by Wayne Cornelius published in the *Population and Development Review* (2002), he noted that the cost of coyote fees affected the percentage of immigrants returning home. When the median cost of a coyote fee was $237, about 50 percent of male Mexican migrants returned home after two years; when it rose to $711, however, that number fell to only 38 percent.

7 THE GROWING INFLUENCE OF MEXICAN AMERICANS

The number of foreign-born residents in the United States grew steadily during the last three decades of the 20th century: from 9.6 million in 1970, to 14.1 million in 1980, to 19.8 million in 1990, before reaching 28.1 million in 2000. That means about 10 percent of the 280 million residents living in the United States were foreign-born at the time of the 2000 Census.

The 2000 Census also indicated that 51.7 percent of this foreign-born population was from Latin America, as compared to 26.4 percent from Asia and 15.8 percent from Europe. The majority of the foreign-born residents from Latin America are Mexican immigrants, many of whom entered the country as undocumented workers.

Need for Immigration Reform

In 2001, President Bush established a task force headed by Secretary of State Colin Powell and Attorney General John Ashcroft to study possible large-scale immigration reform that would address the issue of illegal migration from Mexico. One solution that received public attention was to allow a far greater number of potential workers in Mexico to be able to enter the United States legally and work on temporary visas, rather than enter illegally, often through dangerous terrain. Such a temporary worker program would allow Mexicans to travel back and forth legally while working in the United

◀ Mexican president Vicente Fox and President George W. Bush address the media outside the White House in October 2001. Before the September 2001 terrorist attacks in New York and Washington, D.C., Bush and Fox were holding discussions over loosening immigration laws; after the attacks the U.S. government decided to focus more on border security.

States. The more difficult issue became what to do about the 3 to 4 million undocumented Mexican workers already in America. One discussed solution was to let them become temporary workers as well. They could have a chance at permanent residence (a green card) after they have finished a set period as temporary workers.

Any program that allowed people who had entered the country illegally to stay there generated political opposition in Congress. Yet any proposal that ignored the undocumented immigrants already in the country from Mexico—never mind those here from other countries—also created controversy. This dilemma became a major political issue.

For the most part, the idea of immigration reform was well received. A number of Republicans looked upon the growing Hispanic population as potential supporters of their party and viewed the status quo of the time as unacceptable. Other Republicans said they would oppose any large-scale measure that allowed undocumented immigrants to become permanent residents.

The labor union AFL-CIO has changed the views on immigration held by organized labor at the beginning of the 20th century. In February 2000 it endorsed an amnesty for undocumented workers in the United States and the end of sanctions against employers for hiring the undocumented. The union argued that the current system drove immigrants underground and made them more susceptible to possible exploitation.

In a letter published in the *New York Times*, Mexican president Vicente Fox argued for major reform, explaining that it would benefit both the United States and Mexico:

> Dealing with the migration phenomenon will bring great benefits in both the short and the long term. Working and living conditions would improve for Mexican workers in the United States, disincentives would be created for workers crossing the border without documents, and with the right regional development programs, the Mexican work force could be given economic incentives to stay home, bringing about growth in my country.

President George W. Bush added his support for the concept

of major immigration reform, without committing to specific details. The president said in an August 2001 speech: "If you can make a living in America, and you can't find a job in Mexico, family values don't stop at the southern border. People are coming to work to provide food for their families."

On September 6, 2001, President Fox visited Washington, D.C., with plans to begin negotiations with President Bush and Congress for extensive immigration reform. He urged Congress to consider a measure permitting undocumented immigrants to seek visas. Discussion moved along smoothly, as there appeared to be growing support for significant reforms, but the situation would change a few days later.

Terrorism Tightens the Border

On the bright, blue morning of September 11, 19 non-immigrants on temporary visas who were of Middle Eastern nationality hijacked four jets and used three of them as missiles to destroy the World Trade Center in New York City and a portion of the Pentagon in Arlington, Virginia. With these

President Bush signs the Enhanced Border Security and Visa Entry Reform Act with congressional members in attendance, May 2002. The act, along with the USA PATRIOT Act, was passed in response to the September 2001 terrorist attacks.

attacks, plans for immigration reform with Mexico came to a halt.

In the months that followed, the U.S. government toughened its attitude toward immigration. Moreover, the downturn in the economy made gaining political support for any new worker program difficult. Of utmost importance in future discussions with Mexico, U.S. officials indicated, would be border security. Concerned about the implications of the terrorist attacks on future security, Congress no longer appeared to support the loosening of immigration laws. Most preferred that the borders be tightened further.

Meanwhile, at the border the war on terrorism resulted in increased security, including more vehicle searches and identification checks. Despite the tighter border, undocumented immigrants did not stop attempting dangerous crossings over the border. The question of how to prevent the loss of life while maintaining strong border security remains to be solved.

Continuing Steady Growth

According to the 2000 Census, 20 million Mexicans and Mexican Americans live in the United States—7.3 percent of the total U.S. population. Though Canada is home to far fewer Mexicans, the numbers of immigrants to Canada from Central and South America has jumped sharply, from just 0.6 percent of the foreign-born population before the 1960s to approximately 10 percent of it by the mid-1990s.

Most statisticians agree that these numbers will continue to grow. In fact, they predict that by the year 2050 Hispanics will make up one-quarter of the total U.S. population.

According to a study released in 2002 by Mexico's National Population Council (NPC), an agency of the Ministry of the Interior, immigration to the United States will continue to flow steadily, doubling the Mexican-born U.S. population (which it had estimated as approximately 18 million) by the year 2030. The NPC stated that because Mexico and the United States share a border and are likely to become more and more economically dependent on one another, this stream of migration will remain consistent.

The Population Council stated that changes in Mexico's standard of living alone, such as an improved Mexican economy or reduction in the wage differences between the United States and Mexico, may not lower the migration numbers. In other words, the incentives for Mexicans to immigrate to the United States include not only steady jobs and sources of income, but also dreams of the great prosperity that can be found there.

According to Harvard professor and demographer Marcelo M. Suarez-Orozco, half of the Mexican immigrants who come the United States do so because they want to be with family members who are already living in the country. "Someone said the formula for a happy life is based on love and work," he says. "That's why Mexicans migrate—love of family and to get a good job."

Anxieties that the U.S. economy and the job force would suffer from immigration have not been borne out by history. In the future, the demand for labor across different sets of skills will remain high. In fact, the U.S. Department of Labor estimates that by 2010 there will be more than 20 million jobs created that can be filled by people with minimal education. And by the summer of 2003, several bills had been introduced in Congress to provide temporary worker visas and legalization for Mexicans and other workers.

Growing Influence on American Culture

Hispanics now live in cities across the United States, in every major city and in hundreds of small towns. Every state contains a Latino population, which in some areas continues to rapidly increase.

The U.S. Hispanic population is young. The proportion of Latinos under the age of 18, at 35 percent, is much higher than the national average, which stands at 25 percent. Mexican Americans are the largest of second-generation immigrant groups. As these young Mexican Americans grow up,

Cristina Saralegui is host of *The Cristina Show*, the premier talk show of Univision, a Spanish-language television network. Univision and its rival, Telemundo, compete with other U.S. networks for Mexican American viewers.

they will maintain an expanding influence on social, economic, and political aspects of American society.

Spanish-language media took off as early as the 1980s, with the success of two major television networks, Univision and Telemundo. By July 1999 Univision had became the fifth most-watched broadcast network, surpassing WB and UPN. (The growth was fueled by broadcasts in large Hispanic markets in Los Angeles, New York, Houston, Miami, and Fresno and Bakersfield in California.) Hundreds of Spanish-language radio stations throughout the country speak to millions of Hispanic Americans. Newsstands and libraries offer countless selections of Spanish-language newspapers, magazines, and books.

Hispanics have made inroads into the mainstream media, although at a slow pace, considering the large Latino presence in the American population (13 percent as of 2001). In a 2001 study by Children Now, an advocacy group that evaluates the media, the representation of Latino characters in prime-time television actually dropped from 3 percent to 2 percent during the 1999 and 2000 seasons. To protest the dearth of Latino representation, Hispanic organizations called for a weeklong boycott, or "brownout," of network television in September 1999.

Cable television responded to the boycott with two Latino

shows, *The Brothers Garcia* on Nickelodeon and *Resurrection Blvd.* on Showtime. In 2002, film director Gregory Nava produced *American Family*, a groundbreaking television program that was broadcast on PBS—the first time network television offered a drama based on a Mexican American family.

In the summer of 2003 the first American Latino Television Network in English joined the Dish Network's "America's Top 150" programming package. Entitled SíTV, the Latino-themed network targets the growing market of young second- and third-generation Hispanics, who speak English but hold onto many aspects of their cultural heritage.

Economic Impact

Many other businesses have discovered and are trying to tap into the rapidly growing Hispanic market. Utility companies, banks, and real estate agencies hire bilingual personnel, offer Spanish-language telephone service, and print brochures and pamphlets in both English and Spanish. Many companies specifically target the Hispanic market in television commercials and other forms of advertising. The potential earnings are enormous. According to Enrique Berruga, the undersecretary for foreign affairs in Mexico, the 20 million Mexican immigrants in

Jeff Valdez (back), creator of the children's television show *The Brothers Garcia*, and one of its stars, Alvin Alvarez, greet photographers at an awards ceremony in 2001. Television networks began showing *The Brothers Garcia* and other cable shows featuring Latinos after advocacy groups protested the lack of Latinos represented on prime-time television.

the United States represent at least $450 billion in purchasing power.

While millions of Mexican laborers helped spur the economic growth of the United States over the years, that productive capacity is not the only influence on the U.S. economy. The ever-increasing number of small businesses owned and operated by Latinos has made a major impact as well.

Hispanic-owned retail stores and mini-marts have revitalized many blighted city neighborhoods. For example, shops owned by Latinos line streets that had once been devastated by the 1992 riots in Central Los Angeles. In fact, Los Angeles contains the most Hispanic-owned businesses (mostly by Mexican Americans) of all U.S. cities—more than 200,000 firms as of 1998, according to UCLA's Center for the Study of Latino Health. They account for about one-sixth of all Latino-owned businesses in the United States.

A Growing Political Influence

Mexican Americans have made slow but steady progress in politics. Traditionally, the political affiliation of Hispanics has been with the Democratic Party. Many Mexican Americans in California found it difficult to identify with the Republican Party in the 1990s after Proposition 187. Since then, Republicans have sought to reach out more to the Spanish-speaking community. In May 2001 President George W. Bush became the first U.S. president to deliver his weekly radio address in Spanish. Legislative leaders from both parties are well aware of the potential political clout of the fast-growing Hispanic population.

Since more than a third of Latinos are under the voting age, Hispanic voting power will continue to increase. In California Latinos hold elected office at practically all levels of government, from city hall to the U.S. House of Representatives. In Nevada, where Hispanics make up a fifth of the population, the 63-member state legislature contained only two Latinos in 2001. As Antonio Gonzalez, the president of the Southwest Voter

Registration Education Project told *Time* magazine in June 2001, "We're on the ground floor of political empowerment."

As of the elections of 2002, many politicians, particularly in Florida, New York, California, and Texas, were actively pursuing the Latino vote. Adam Segal, editor of the *Johns Hopkins Journal of American Politics*, estimated that candidates spent at least $8 million pitching themselves on more than 12,000 Spanish-language advertisements. Instead of direct translation of English to Spanish, scripts for ads featured music and messages specifically tailored for the Hispanic viewer. Usually upbeat, unlike the negative English-language commercials, these political ads usually focused on issues thought to be of interest to Latinos: family, education, and employment.

Mexican immigration to the United States has a long history, one that is likely to continue many years into the future. Mexico will also likely remain the leading source of legal immigrants to the United States and, barring major U.S. policy changes and significant economic improvement in Mexico, undocumented Mexicans will continue to attempt entry into America. Mexicans will continue to make sacrifices and take risks to achieve a better life north of the border for themselves and their families. Whether the United States and Mexico will reach a lasting agreement on migration cannot be known. What can be known is that such an accord would write a new chapter for Mexican immigration to the United States.

FAMOUS MEXICAN AMERICANS/CANADIANS

Joan Baez (1941–), celebrated singer and guitarist who achieved popularity during the 1960s and '70s; also a political activist and advocate for nonviolent protest.

César E. Chávez (1927–93), activist for migrant workers' rights and social justice for the Latino community; cofounder of the United Farmworkers Union (1962). Awarded the Presidential Medal of Freedom posthumously in 1994; commemorated on U.S. postage stamp in 2003.

Linda Chavez (1947–), president of the Center for Equal Opportunity, a public policy research organization based in Washington, D.C.; author of *Out of the Barrio: Toward a New Politics of Hispanic Assimilation* and a political analyst for the TV network Fox.

Linda Chavez-Thompson (1944–), labor leader; national vice-president of the Labor Council for Latin American Advancement between 1986 and 1996; executive vice president of the AFL-CIO.

Henry G. Cisneros (1947–), first Mexican American U.S. secretary of housing and urban development (1993–97); served as mayor of San Antonio, Texas (elected in 1981).

Sandra Cisneros (1954–), writer of Chicana novels (*The House on Mango Street*, *Caramelo*), poetry (*My Wicked Wicked Ways*), and short stories (*Woman Hollering Creek and Other Stories*).

Ernesto Garaza (1905–84), political activist and scholar specializing in Latin American studies; worked to improve the conditions and treatment of Mexican farm laborers and urban workers; authored Chicano autobiography *Barrio Boy* (1971), the story of his and his family's immigration to the United States.

Henry B. González (1916–2000), first Mexican American to serve in Texas state senate in 100 years (elected in 1956); elected to U.S. House of Representatives, where he served longer than any other Hispanic (1961–98); first Mexican American from Texas in a national office. Cofounded Hispanic Congressional Caucus.

Salma Hayek (1968–), acclaimed actress featured in *Desperado*, 1995; *From Dusk till Dawn*, 1996; *Fools Rush In*, 1997; *54*, 1998; *The Faculty*, 1998; *Dogma*, 1999; *Timecode*, 2000; and *Frida*, 2002. Received Blockbuster Entertainment Award, Favorite Supporting Actress in an Action Film, for *Wild Wild West*, 1999; and Golden Globe and Oscar nomination for Best Actress in *Frida*, 2002.

FAMOUS MEXICAN AMERICANS/CANADIANS

Oscar de la Hoya (1973–), super welterweight boxer and Olympic gold-medal winner (1992); has won world championships in five different weight classes.

Francisco Jiménez (1943–), writer and editor of Mexico-themed books for adults and children, including a collection of short stories based on his life: *The Circuit: Stories from the Life of a Migrant Child*.

Mario Molina (1943–), Massachusetts Institute of Technology professor of Earth, Atmospheric, and Planetary Sciences; winner of 1995 Nobel Prize in Chemistry for work in research for atmospheric chemistry, particularly the formation and depletion of ozone in the atmosphere.

Gregory Nava (1949–), screenwriter and film director. Acclaimed for the Oscar-nominated film *El Norte* (1984, which relates the story of a Mexican brother and sister who immigrate to the United States). Other directorial films include *Mi Familia/My Family* (1995), *Selena* (1997), *Why Do Fools Fall in Love* (1998), and *Killing Pablo* (2002).

Edward James Olmos (1947–), actor, filmmaker, political activist. Acclaimed in the 1980s for his Emmy Award–winning role on television series *Miami Vice*; nominated for an Oscar for his role in 1988 film *Stand and Deliver*, which tells the true story of a Hispanic math teacher who inspires his students. Director of films including *American Me* (1992) and *Jack and Marilyn* (2002).

Derek Parra (1970–), long-track speed skater who became first Mexican American to win a gold medal at the Winter Olympics (2002).

Frederico Peña (1947–), mayor of Denver, Colorado; U.S. secretary of transportation (1993–97); secretary of energy (1997–98).

Selena Quintanilla Perez (1971–95), popular singer born in Lake Jackson, Texas, whose rising career was cut short when she was murdered at age 23; in 1993 *Selena Live* received a Grammy Award for Best Mexican American album. Another Grammy-nominated album, *Amor Prohibido*, was released in 1994.

Anthony Rudolph Oaxaca Quinn (1915–2001), Oscar-winning actor (for *Viva Zapata!* in 1952) who appeared in more than 200 films during a 60-year acting career; remembered for roles in *Zorba the Greek* and *Lawrence of Arabia*.

FAMOUS MEXICAN AMERICANS/CANADIANS

Linda Ronstadt (1946–), acclaimed singer; developed a large following during the 1970s and '80s; has recorded 12 platinum and 17 gold albums, including a 1987 album of traditional Mexican and Spanish songs, *Canciones de Mi Padre*.

Edward R. Roybal (1916–), Congressman from California for more than 30 years (1963–93); cofounded Hispanic Congressional Caucus (1976); first Mexican American since 1881 to win a seat on the Los Angeles City Council (elected in 1949). As member of U.S. House of Representatives, authored first bilingual education bill and fostered legislation to provide access to bilingual proceedings in U.S. courts.

Carlos Santana (1947–), talented guitarist whose recordings of Latin-flavored rock music have charted for decades, beginning with the Santana Blues Band in 1966; winner of 8 Grammy Awards; inducted into the Rock and Roll Hall of Fame in 1998.

Luis Valdez (1940–), playwright and film director; called "father of Chicano theater"; founded El Teatro Campesino in 1965, a touring theater troupe that dramatized the plight of migrant farmworkers; writer, producer, and director of plays such as *Zoot Suit* (1978), which was later adapted into a movie; wrote and directed the film *La Bamba* (1987).

GLOSSARY

barrio—a neighborhood of Spanish-speaking residents; from the Spanish word for "suburb" or "township."

bracero—the Spanish word for "hired hand."

Californio—a Mexican American native to California.

Chicano—a Mexican American (first used during the 1960s as a source of ethnic identity).

colonias—slums and shantytowns that sprang up in Mexico's border towns.

coyote—in the context of immigration, a smuggler paid to guide illegal immigrants across the Mexico-U.S. border.

deport—to forcibly remove someone from a country, usually back to his or her native land.

El norte—Spanish for "the North"; usually refers to the United States.

green card—a document that denotes permanent residence in the United States.

Hispanic—a person of Spanish or Latino descent.

maquiladora—an assembly plant, also called "*maquila*."

matricula consular—a Mexican identity card.

mestizo—a person of mixed Native American and Spanish ancestry.

migrant laborer—an agricultural worker who travels from region to region, taking on short-term jobs.

naturalization—the act of granting a foreign-born person citizenship.

passport—a paper or book that identifies the holder as the citizen of a country; usually required for traveling to or through other foreign lands.

pollos—Spanish word for "chicken"; refers to a coyote's customer.

quinceañera—a Mexican celebration of a teenage girl's 15th birthday.

La raza—"the people"; refers specifically to the people of Mexico.

Tejano—a Mexican American native to Texas.

visa—official authorization that permits arrival at a port of entry but does not guarantee admission into the United States.

FURTHER READING

Annerino, John. *Dead in Their Tracks: Crossing America's Desert Borderlands*. New York: Four Walls Eight Windows, 1999.

Dudley, William, ed. *Illegal Immigration*. San Diego, Calif.: Greenhaven Press, 2002.

Garcia, Alma. *The Mexican Americans*. Westport, Conn.: Greenwood Press, 2002.

Gonzales, Manuel. *Mexicanos: A History of Mexicans in the United States.* Bloomington and Indianapolis: Indiana University Press, 1999.

Hart, Elva Treviño. *Barefoot Heart: Stories of a Migrant Child.* Tempe, Ariz.: Bilingual Press/Editorial Bilingüe, 1999.

Martinez, Rubén. *Crossing Over: A Mexican Family on the Migrant Trail*. New York: Metropolitan Books, 2001.

Massey, Douglas S., Jorge Durand, and Nolan J. Maloone. *Beyond Smoke and Mirrors: Mexican Immigration in an Era of Economic Integration*. New York: Russell Sage Foundation, 2002.

http://www.latinousa.org/

This site gives listings and descriptions of shows on *Latino USA*, the only "national, English-language radio program produced from a Latino perspective."

http://www.maldef.org/index.cfm

The home site of this nonprofit advocacy group covers news and events and provides educational and employment services to Mexican Americans.

http://www.lulac.org/

LULAC is the oldest Hispanic organization in the U.S. Its homepage provides useful information on the organization's programs as well as a comprehensive list of links to other sites.

http://www.mfacmchicago.org/index.htm

This museum is the largest Mexican and Latino arts institution in the United States, located in Chicago. The site offers updates on the latest exhibitions.

http://www.nclr.org/

This website, sponsored by another advocacy group, presents valuable commentary on Mexican American political issues and the latest news on current events and social programs.

INDEX

agriculture industry, 23–24, *62*,
    63–64
    in Mexico, 32–33, 35–36
Agua Prieta, Mex., *15*, 57
Alien Registration Receipt Card Form I-
    151 (green card), 65
Alvarez, Alvin, *97*
American Enterprise, 74–75
American Family, 96–97
American GI Forum, 64
amnesty program, 51–52
    See also Immigration Reform and
    Control Act (1986)
Anaya, Rodolfo A., 22
Antorcha Guadalupana, 71–72
    See also holidays
Apodaca, Jerry, 21
Arizona, 21, 55–57, 59, 60
Ashcroft, John, 91
assimilation, 74–76
    See also Mexican Americans

Baez, Joan, 100
Berruga, Enrique, 97
bilingual education, 83–85, 87
Bilingual Education Act (1968), 84
border crossing deaths, *56*, 79, *80*,
    81–83
    See also undocumented
    immigrants
braceros. *See* migrant workers
The Brothers Garcia, 96, *97*
Brownsville, Tex., 27, 55, 57, 79
Bureau of Citizenship and Immigration
    Services (BCIS), 45
    See also Immigration and
    Naturalization Service (INS)
Bureau of Customs and Border
    Protection (BCBP), *39*, 44
Bureau of Immigration and Customs
    Enforcement (BICE), 44–45
Bush, George H. W., 22, 31, 92–93
Bush, George W., 91, 98

Calexico, Calif., 49, 55, *82*

California, 21, 59, 87, 98
Canada, 60, 75
    immigration history, 46–50
    Mexican population in, 15, *16*, 94
Castillo, Ana, 22
Castro, Raul, 21
Center for the Study of Latino Health, 98
Chávez, César, 20, 24, 100
Chavez, Linda, 74, 100
Chavez-Thompson, Linda, 100
Chicago, *59*, 60
Chicano movement, 17, 20, 22
    See also Mexican Americans
Chinese Exclusion Act of 1882, 39
Cinco de Mayo (May 5), 69, *70*, *71*
Cisneros, Henry G., 21–22, 100
Cisneros, Sandra, 22, 100
Ciudad Juárez, Mex., 57
Cornelius, Wayne, 89
coyotes (smugglers), 79–81, 89
    See also undocumented
    immigrants

demographics, Mexican American,
    17–18, 35, 95
Department of Homeland Security, *39*,
    44–45
Department of Justice, 44
Diaz, Luis, 49
Diego, Juan, 71, *72*, 73
discrimination, 65
Displaced Persons Act of 1948, 41
Douglas, Ariz., 55, 80
dual nationality, 73
Durand, Jorge, 35

economy, 23–25, 97–98
    in Mexico, 27–36, 53, 63, 95
education, bilingual, 83–85, 87
Ejército Zapatista Nacional (EZLN), *32*,
    33
El Paso, Tex., 57, 59
employment, 23–25, 50, 51, 55–56,
    63–64, 65, 75, 91, 95, 97–98
    in maquiladoras, *27*, 28–29

Numbers in **bold italic** refer to captions.

English as a Second Language
    (ESL), *84*, 85
    See also bilingual education
Enhanced Border Security and Visa
    Entry Reform Act (2002), 43, *93*
ethnicity, 19, 39–40
    See also quotas

family life, 68–69
Feast Day of Our Lady of Guadalupe
    (December 12), 71–73
    See also holidays
Fermi, Laura, 40
Fox, Vicente, *34*, 35, 76–77, *91*, 92–93
Frida, *22*

Gadsden Purchase, 33
Garaza, Ernesto, 100
García, Hector P., 64
Gonzales, Rodolfo ("Corky"), 22
Gonzalez, Antonio, 98
González, Henry B., 21, 100
Grant, Madison, 40
green card, 65
Guanajuato, 35, *36*

Hayek, Salma, *22*, 23, 100
Hidalgo, Miguel, 69
Higuera, Ted, 23
Hispanic Congressional Caucus, 21
Hispanics, 17, 94
    See also Mexican Americans
holidays, 68–73, 87–88
    See also religion
Homeland Security Act (2002), 43
Hoya, Oscar de La, 23, 101
Huerta, Delores, 24

I Am Joaquin (Gonzales), 22
illegal immigrants. *See* undocumented
    immigrants
Illegal Immigration Reform and
    Immigrant Responsibility Act
    (1996), 43
immigration
    acts, 40, 41, 42, 43, 47, 48–49, 51–53

difficulties of, 74–76, 79–83
history of, in Canada, 46–50
history of, in the United States,
    39–46, 51–53, 99
rates, 19, *20*, 24–25, 35, 39, 41,
    44, 45–46, 51, 94–95
reform, *34*, 91–94
Immigration and Naturalization Service
    (INS), 43, 45, 49, 50, 52, 53, 80
Independence Day (September 16),
    69, *70*
    See also holidays

Jacoby, Tamar, 75
Jalisco, 35, *36*
Jiménez, Francisco, 22, 101
*Johns Hopkins Journal of American
    Politics*, 99
Johnson, Lyndon, *42*
Juárez, Benito, Gen., 69, *71*

Kahlo, Frida, *22*

Lafata, Joe, 56
LaMonica, Consuelo, 73
language barrier, 74–76
    See also bilingual education
Laredo, Tex., 57, 59, *61*, *88*
Latin American Research Review, 35, 87
Latinos, 17
    See also Mexican Americans
Laughlin, Harry N., 40
League of United Latin American
    Citizens (LULAC), 64–65
Legal Immigration Family Equity Act
    (LIFE), 52
Longoria, Félix, 64
Los Angeles, 59, 96, 98
Lujan, Manuel, Jr., 22

maquiladoras, *27*, 28–29, 56
    See also employment
Massey, Douglas S., 35
Matamoros, Mex., 55, 57, 79
matricula consular, 85
McAllen, Tex., 57

INDEX

Mexicali, Mex., 55
Mexican Americans
  culture, 20–21, 22–23, 68–73, 76,
    95–96
  demographics, 17–18, 35, 95
  discrimination against, 65
  dual nationality, 73
  and the economy, 23–25, 97–98
  employment, 23–25, 50, 51, 55–56,
    63–64, 65, 75, 91, 95, 97–98
  family life, 68–69
  political involvement, 20–22,
    98–99
  population, 15, 17, 18–19, 59–63,
    91, 94
  reasons for immigrating, 27–28,
    30, 36–37
  return migration, 87–89
  support agencies for, 64–65, 67,
    73
Mexican War, 33
Mexico, 15–17
  economy, 27–36, 53, 63, 95
  government, 30, 35
  population, 29
Mexico City, 27, *28*, 59, 71–72, *87*
Michoacán, 35, *36*
migrant workers, 24, 35, *62*, 63
  See also employment
Minister of Citizenship and Immigration
  Canada, 48
Molina, Mario, 101
Mulroney, Brian, 31

Naco, Ariz., 55
Naco, Mex., 55
NAFTA. *See* North American Free Trade
  Agreement (NAFTA)
National Council of La Raza, 64
National Farmworkers Association
  (NFWA), 24
  See also Chávez, César
National Geographic, 37, 49
National Population Council (NPC),
  94–95
naturalization rates, *60*, 75

Nava, Gregory, 96, 101
Nevada, 59
New Mexico, 21, 60
New River, 82
New York, 59
New York City, *59*, 60, 71–72, 96
Nogales, Ariz., 55–56
Nogales, Mex., 55
North American Free Trade Agreement
  (NAFTA), 30–32,
  35–36
  See also economy
North Carolina, 59
Nuevo Laredo, Mex., 57

Office for Mexicans Living Abroad,
  76–77
Olmos, Edward James, 23, 101
Operation Gatekeeper, *56*, 57, 82
Operation Hold the Line, *56*, 57
Operation Wetback, 50–51
  See also undocumented
  immigrants
Ortega, Katherine, 22

Parfit, Michael, 49
Parra, Derek, 23, 101
Partido Acción Nacional (PAN), 35
Partido Revolucionario Institucional
  (PRI), 30, 35
Pearson, Lester, 47
Peña, Frederico, *22*, 101
Perez, Selena Quintanilla. *See* Selena
petroleum, 30
  See also economy
political involvement, 20–22, 98–99
population
  Hispanic, 17
  Mexican Americans, 15, 17,
    18–19, 59–63, 91, 94
  Mexico, 16, 29
Powell, Colin, 91
Proposition 187, 53, 98
Proposition 227, 87
  See also bilingual education

INDEX

Quinn, Anthony Rudolph Oaxaca, 101
quotas, 41–42, 48
    See also immigration

Reagan, Ronald, 22, 51, **52**
Refugee Act of 1980, 43
refugees, 41, 43, 47, 48
religion, 17, 70–73, 76
Resurrection Blvd., 96
Reyes, Belinda, 88–89
Reynosa, Mex., 57
Rivera, Diego, 67, **68**
Rodriguez, Richard, 22
Roman Catholicism. *See* religion
Ronstadt, Linda, 102
Roybal, Edward R., 21, 102

Sack, Kevin, 62–63
Salinas de Gotari, Carlos, 30–31
San Antonio, Tex., 22, 59, 60
San Cristobal de Las Casas, **32**, 33
San Diego, Calif., *18*, *54*, 55, 60, 82, **83**
San Luis, Mex., 55
Sanchez, George Isidore, 84
Santa Ana, Calif., **67**
Santana, Carlos, 23, 102
Saralegui, Cristina, **96**
Scully, C. D., 40
Segal, Adam, 99
Selena, 23, 101
sister cities, **50**, 55, 57
    See also undocumented
        immigrants
Smith, James, 65
Suarez-Orozco, Marcelo M., 95

Telemundo, 67, 96
Temporary Quota Act of 1921, 40
    See also quotas
terrorism, 43, **91**, 93–94
Texas, 21, 57, 59, 60
Tijuana, Mex., *18*, 27, **54**, 55, 82
Treaty of Guadalupe Hidalgo, 33
Truman, Harry, 41

undocumented immigrants, *18*, 19, *31*,
    32, 36–37, 43, 45, 49, 51–57, 79–83,
    89, 91–92
    See also immigration
United Farmworkers (UFW), 24
United States
    economy, 23–25, 95, 97–98
    immigration history, 39–46,
        51–53, 99
Univision, 67, 96
USA PATRIOT Act (2002), 43, **93**

Valdez, Jeff, **97**
Valdez, Luis, 102
Valenzela, Fernando, 23
visas, 43, 45, 91, 93
    See also immigration

Wilson, Pete, 53
World War I, 40
World War II, 40, 41, 47, 64

Yuma, Ariz., 55

Zedillo, Ernesto, 30, 33
Zenteno, René M., 35

CONTRIBUTORS

SENATOR EDWARD M. KENNEDY has represented Massachusetts in the United States Senate for more than 40 years. Kennedy serves on the Senate Judiciary Committee, where he is the senior Democrat on the Immigration Subcommittee. He currently is the ranking member on the Health, Education, Labor and Pensions Committee in the Senate, and also serves on the Armed Services Committee, where he is a member of the Senate Arms Control Observer Group. He is also a member of the Congressional Friends of Ireland and a trustee of the John F. Kennedy Center for the Performing Arts in Washington, D.C.

Throughout his career, Kennedy has fought for issues that benefit the citizens of Massachusetts and the nation, including the effort to bring quality health care to every American, education reform, raising the minimum wage, defending the rights of workers and their families, strengthening the civil rights laws, assisting individuals with disabilities, fighting for cleaner water and cleaner air, and protecting and strengthening Social Security and Medicare for senior citizens.

Kennedy is the youngest of nine children of Joseph P. and Rose Fitzgerald Kennedy, and is a graduate of Harvard University and the University of Virginia Law School. His home is in Hyannis Port, Massachusetts, where he lives with his wife, Victoria Reggie Kennedy, and children, Curran and Caroline. He also has three grown children, Kara, Edward Jr., and Patrick, and four grandchildren.

Senior consulting editor STUART ANDERSON served as Executive Associate Commissioner for Policy and Planning and Counselor to the Commissioner at the Immigration and Naturalization Service from August 2001 until January 2003. He spent four and a half years on Capitol Hill on the Senate Immigration Subcommittee, first for Senator Spencer Abraham and then as Staff Director of the subcommittee for Senator Sam Brownback. Prior to that, he was Director of Trade and Immigration Studies at the Cato Institute in Washington, D.C., where he produced reports on the history of immigrants in the military and the role of immigrants in high technology. He currently serves as Executive Director of the National Foundation for American Policy, a nonpartisan public policy research organization focused on trade, immigration, international relations. He has an M.A. from Georgetown University and a B.A. in Political Science from Drew University. His articles have appeared in such publications as the *Wall Street Journal*, *New York Times*, and *Los Angeles Times*.

MARIAN L. SMITH served as the senior historian of the U.S. Immigration and Naturalization Service (INS) from 1988 to 2003, and is currently the immigration and naturalization historian within the Department of Homeland Security in Washington, D.C. She studies, publishes, and speaks on the history of the immigration agency and is active in the management of official 20th-century immigration records.

PETER HAMMERSCHMIDT is the First Secretary (Financial and Military Affairs) for the Permanent Mission of Canada to the United Nations. Before taking this position, he was a ministerial speechwriter and policy specialist for the Department of National

Defence in Ottawa. Prior to joining the public service, he served as the Publications Director for the Canadian Institute of Strategic Studies in Toronto. He has a B.A. (Honours) in Political Studies from Queen's University, and an MScEcon in Strategic Studies from the University of Wales, Aberystwyth. He currently lives in New York, where in his spare time he operates a freelance editing and writing service, Wordschmidt Communications.

Manuscript reviewer ESTHER OLAVARRIA serves as General Counsel to Senator Edward M. Kennedy, ranking Democrat on the U.S. Senate Judiciary Committee, Subcommittee on Immigration. She is Senator Kennedy's primary advisor on immigration, nationality, and refugee legislation and policies. Prior to her current job, she practiced immigration law in Miami, Florida, working at several nonprofit organizations. She cofounded the Florida Immigrant Advocacy Center and served as managing attorney, supervising the direct service work of the organization and assisting in the advocacy work. She also worked at Legal Services of Greater Miami, as the directing attorney of the American Immigration Lawyers Association Pro Bono Project, and at the Haitian Refugee Center, as a staff attorney. She clerked for a Florida state appellate court after graduating from the University of Florida Law School. She was born in Havana, Cuba, and raised in Florida.

Reviewer JANICE V. KAGUYUTAN is Senator Edward M. Kennedy's advisor on immigration, nationality, and refugee legislation and policies. Prior to working on Capitol Hill, Ms. Kaguyutan was a staff attorney at the NOW Legal Defense and Education Fund's Immigrant Women Program. Ms. Kaguyutan has written and trained extensively on the rights of immigrant victims of domestic violence, sexual assault, and human trafficking. Her previous work includes representing battered immigrant women in civil protection order, child support, divorce, and custody hearings, as well as representing immigrants before the Immigration and Naturalization Service on a variety of immigration matters.

LEEANNE GELLETLY is a freelance writer and editor living outside Philadelphia, Pennsylvania. She has written biographies of Harriet Beecher Stowe and Mae Jemison, and geography books on South American countries.

PICTURE CREDITS